Plant Invaders of Mid-Atlantic Natural Areas
FIELD GUIDE

Lead Author
Jil M. Swearingen

Co-Author
Judith P. Fulton

Citation
Swearingen, J.M. and J.P. Fulton. 2022. Plant Invaders of Mid-Atlantic Natural Areas, Field Guide. Passiflora Press. 200 pp.

© Jil Swearingen 2022. No claim is made to public domain works. All rights reserved.

ISBN 978-0-578-99147-4

For Copies
Print: info@maipc.org
Digital: invasive.org/midatlantic/fieldguide

Layout/Print Production
E.C. Fisher Design

Cover Photo
Autumn-olive (*Elaeagnus umbellata*) © Bill Johnson

ACKNOWLEDGMENTS

Contributors
Melanie Schori—Taxonomic nomenclature
Nancy Rybicki—Water chestnut

Editorial Reviewers
Ashley Fulton-Howard
Selma Sawaya

Scientific Reviewers
E. M. Barrows
Kathy Bilton
Bethany Bradley
Ana Chuquin
Charlie Davis
Lynde Dodd
Sam Droege
Michael Ellis
Hess Muse
Mike Naylor
Paul Peterson
Ian Pfingsten
Rod Simmons
Douglas Tallamy
Aleksandra Voznitza
Alan Whittemore
Lewis Ziska

Photographers
Lynde Dodd, US Army Engineer & Research Development Center
Peter M. Dziuk, MinnesotaWildflowers.info
Michael Ellis, University of Maryland
Chris Evans, University of Illinois
Judy Fulton, EcoPlant Consulting
Bill Harms, Patuxent Research Refuge Plant Inventory Project
Bill Johnson, billjohnsonbeyondbutterflies.com
Mic Julien, The Commonwealth Scientific and Industrial Research Organisation
Wayne Longbottom
Graves Lovell, Alabama Department of Conservation & Natural Resources
Leslie J. Mehrhoff, University of Connecticut
Blythe Merritt
Maria Cristina Niciporciukas
Thomas Palmer, Wetlands Consulting
Amy Richard, University of Florida
Jil Swearingen, In the Weeds Consulting
Douglas Tallamy, University of Delaware
Robert Vidéki, Doronicum Kft.
Amanda Wray

All photographs used with permission.

Contents

Preface 7

Introduction 8
Invasive Species Overview 8
Climate Change & Invasive Plants 15
Restoring Nature at Home 18
Physiographic Provinces & Ecoregions 22

Invasive Plant Summaries 24

Aquatic Invasive Plants 26
Hydrilla (*Hydrilla verticillata*) 27
Parrot-feather (*Myriophyllum aquaticum*) 29
Eurasian watermilfoil (*Myriophyllum spicatum*) 31
Giant salvinia (*Salvinia molesta*) 32
Water chestnut 34
  Two-horned water chestnut (*Trapa bispinosa* var. *iinumai*)
  Eurasian water chestnut (*Trapa natans*)

Terrestrial Invasive Plants 38
GRASSES & SEDGES
Joint-head grass (*Arthraxon hispidus*) 40
Chinese fountain grass (*Cenchrus purpurascens*) 41
Japanese stiltgrass (*Microstegium vimineum*) 43
Chinese silver grass (*Miscanthus sinensis*) 45
Wavyleaf basketgrass (*Oplismenus undulatifolius*) 47
European common reed (*Phragmites australis* ssp. *australis*) 48
Bamboo 50
  Golden bamboo (*Phyllostachys aurea*)
  Yellow-groove bamboo (*Phyllostachys aureosulcata*)
  Bisset bamboo (*Phyllostachys bissetii*)
  Arrow bamboo (*Pseudosasa japonica*)
Bog bulrush (*Schoenoplectiella mucronata*) 53
Ravenna grass (*Tripidium ravennae*) 55

FORBS

Garlic mustard (*Alliaria petiolata*) 57
Italian arum (*Arum italicum*) 59
Spotted knapweed (*Centaurea stoebe* ssp. *australis*) 61
Canada thistle (*Cirsium arvense*) 63
Incised fumewort (*Corydalis incisa*) 64
Mulberry-weed (*Fatoua villosa*) 66
Fig buttercup (*Ficaria verna*) 67
Ground ivy (*Glechoma hederacea*) 69
Orange daylily (*Hemerocallis fulva*) 70
Dame's rocket (*Hesperis matronalis*) 71
Sericea lespedeza (*Lespedeza cuneata*) 73
Purple loosestrife (*Lythrum salicaria*) 74
Marsh dewflower (*Murdannia keisak*) 76
Star-of-Bethlehem 77
  Nodding star-of-Bethlehem (*Ornithogalum nutans*)
  Garden star-of-Bethlehem (*Ornithogalum umbellatum*)
Beefsteak plant (*Perilla frutescens*) 79
Asian jumpseed (*Persicaria filiformis*) 80
Mock strawberry (*Potentilla indica*) 83
Japanese knotweed (*Reynoutria japonica*) 84
European stinging nettle (*Urtica dioica* ssp. *dioica*) 86

SHRUBS

Japanese angelica tree (*Aralia elata*) 88
Japanese barberry (*Berberis thunbergii*) 90
Autumn-olive (*Elaeagnus umbellata*) 92
Winged burning bush (*Euonymus alatus*) 94
Privet 96
  Border privet (*Ligustrum obtusifolium*)
  Garden privet (*Ligustrum ovalifolium*)
  Chinese privet (*Ligustrum sinense*)
  European privet (*Ligustrum vulgare*)
Amur honeysuckle (*Lonicera maackii*) 98
Morrow's honeysuckle (*Lonicera morrowii*) 100
Leatherleaf mahonia (*Mahonia bealei*) 102
Multiflora rose (*Rosa multiflora*) 103

Wineberry (*Rubus phoenicolasius*) 105
Japanese meadowsweet (*Spiraea japonica*) 107
Asian Viburnums 108
   Linden viburnum (*Viburnum dilatatum*)
   Japanese snowball (*Viburnum plicatum*)
   Double-file viburnum (*Viburnum plicatum* var. *tomentosum*)
   Tea viburnum (*Viburnum setigerum*)
   Siebold viburnum (*Viburnum sieboldii*)

TREES

Norway maple (*Acer platanoides*) 111
Tree-of-heaven (*Ailanthus altissimus*) 112
Silktree (*Albizia julibrissin*) 114
Paper mulberry (*Broussonetia papyrifera*) 115
White mulberry (*Morus alba*) 117
Princess tree (*Paulownia tomentosa*) 119
Callery pear (*Pyrus calleryana*) 121
Sawtooth oak (*Quercus acutissima*) 123

VINES

Chocolate vine (*Akebia quinata*) 125
Porcelain-berry (*Ampelopsis glandulosa* var. *brevipedunculata*) 126
Asian bittersweet (*Celastrus orbiculatus*) 128
Sweet autumn clematis (*Clematis terniflora*) 130
Wintercreeper (*Euonymus fortunei*) 131
English ivy (*Hedera helix*) 133
Japanese hop (*Humulus japonicus*) 135
Japanese honeysuckle (*Lonicera japonica*) 137
Mile-a-minute (*Persicaria perfoliata*) 138
Kudzu (*Pueraria montana* var. *lobata*) 140
Common periwinkle (*Vinca minor*) 142
Black swallow-wort (*Vincetoxicum nigrum*) 143
Pale swallow-wort (*Vincetoxicum rossicum*) 145
Asian Wisterias 147
   Japanese wisteria (*Wisteria floribunda*)
   Hybrid wisteria (*Wisteria* x *formosa*)
   Chinese wisteria (*Wisteria sinensis*)

Other Invasive Plants 151

FORBS

Goutweed (*Aegopodium podagraria*) 151
Broadleaf helleborine (*Epipactis helleborine*) 152
Giant hogweed (*Heracleum mantegazzianum*) 153
Spanish bluebells (*Hyacinthoides hispanica*) 154
Yellow archangel (*Lamium galeobdolon*) 154
Summer-snowflake (*Leucojum aestivum*) 155

SHRUBS

Butterflybush (*Buddleja davidii*) 156
Castor-aralia (*Kalopanax septemlobus*) 156
Jetbead (*Rhodotypos scandens*) 157

TREES

Amur corktree (*Phellodendron amurense*) 158

VINES

Chinese yam (*Dioscorea polystachya*) 158

Control Methods 160

Native Plants for Landscapes 168
Grasses 170
Sedges 171
Ferns 172
Forbs 173
Shrubs 177
Trees 182
Vines 186

References 188

Index to Invasive Plants 198

Preface

The main reason for writing *Plant Invaders of Mid-Atlantic Natural Areas, Field Guide* is to promote native biodiversity. Invasive species, habitat destruction, and global climate change are leading causes of environmental degradation and loss of biological diversity worldwide. The activities of modern people and the inexorable growth of the global human population are responsible for these problems. International trade and travel continue to introduce non-native animals, plants, and pathogens to the United States, some of which threaten our economy, our ecosystems, and our health. It is crucial that we intercept, eradicate and manage invasive species, protect and restore native plant communities, and take urgent steps to reverse the precipitous decline of native insect populations.

According to the *Invasive Plant Atlas of the United States*, there are almost 1,600 invasive plant species in natural areas throughout the U.S. In the mid-Atlantic region, there are more than 600 invasive plant species, according to the *Mid-Atlantic Invaders Tool* (MAIT). *Plant Invaders of Mid-Atlantic Natural Areas, Field Guide* features 92 species of invasive plants, representing about a sixth of the total number known for the region. The species were selected from a long list of established invasives with known significant ecological impacts, as well as some newly emerging species of concern. Unfortunately, many of these invasive plants continue to be grown and sold by the nursery trade.

Plant Invaders provides an introduction to invasive plants affecting mid-Atlantic natural areas, including native origin, current distribution, ecological impacts, methods of spread, identifying features, and suggestions for control. The book provides current scientific plant names; three new introductory sections (Climate Change & Invasive Plants, Restoring Nature at Home, and Physiographic Provinces & Ecoregions); an expanded Native Plants for Landscapes section, and a consolidated Control Method section. Eleven new invasive species have been added: two-horned water chestnut, Chinese fountain grass, Bisset bamboo, incised fumewort, mulberry-weed, Asian jumpseed, mock strawberry, and four Asian viburnum species.

Use this book as an introduction to invasive plants to help you recognize, report, prevent, control and teach others about them. As Dr. Robert E. Eplee, Sr. often preached, *"Spread the word, not the weed!"*

Introduction

Diverse native spring ephemeral plant community in Maryland's Piedmont

INVASIVE SPECIES OVERVIEW

The Importance of Biodiversity

Biological diversity refers collectively to all life forms on Earth and their genetic variation, which enables them to adapt, evolve, and persist in a changing world. Living organisms have evolved in various places on the planet in response to atmospheric, geologic, hydrologic, climatic, and other conditions, as well as interactions with other species, over millions of years. These complex interactions have formed the natural ecosystems and plant communities present today.

The United States has an incredible array of wild natural areas including prairies, deserts, swamps, bogs, marshes, rivers, streams, lakes, forests, and mountain habitats. Our national parks, forests, wildlife refuges, nature preserves, and other protected lands are examples of complex communities and species assemblages, and collectively provide a showcase for native biodiversity. These and other unprotected natural areas are being adversely affected by the introduction and spread of non-native plants, animals and pathogens.

Native, Non-native & Invasive Species

In order to understand the invasive species problem, it is essential to understand the meaning of **native**, **non-native**, and **invasive**.

A **native** or indigenous species is one that occurs in a particular environment without human intervention. Species native to North America are generally recognized as those occurring on the continent prior to European settlement.

A **non-native**, alien, or exotic species is one that has been moved by people from its native range to a new environment rather than dispersed by natural means. Native range includes other continents, ecosystems, and habitats; natural dispersal is by air, water, and wildlife. Many non-native plants have great economic value for agriculture, forestry, horticulture, and other industries, and pose little environmental risk. However, most alien plants are harmful to wildlife because they do not provide the insect food or the nutritious fruits that native animals need for survival.

An **invasive** species is a non-native organism whose introduction causes or is likely to cause economic or environmental harm, or harm to human, animal, or plant health (Executive Order 13751, 2016). Invasive species benefit immensely from arriving in new environments without the natural controls (e.g., herbivores, parasites, and pathogens) found in their native ranges that would help to keep them in check.

CHARACTERISTICS OF INVASIVE PLANTS

- Grow well in disturbed areas
- Are habitat generalists
- Tolerate environmental extremes (e.g., drought, saturated soils, and fire)
- Lack herbivores and pathogens that serve to check their growth
- Reach reproductive age early
- Produce abundant long-lived and viable seeds
- Spread vegetatively by plant fragments, rhizomes, stolons, or tubers
- Provide little food value for native birds and other wildlife
- Have longer photosynthetic periods (e.g., leaf out ahead of natives, lose leaves later in autumn, or maintain foliage through winter)

Costs of invasive species

According to estimates by Crowl et al. 2008 and Pimentel et al. 2005, the annual cost of invasive species in the U.S. is $120 billion. This total includes reduced productivity and sales from agricultural and forest products; impaired use of waterways and terrestrial habitats; harm to the health of people and animals; lower property values; and costs related to monitoring, preventing, controlling, and regulating invasive species. Of the $120 billion, invasive plants cost the U.S. approximately $35 billion each year.

Invasive plants harm natural areas

Like an invading human army, invasive plants are taking over natural ecosystems, pushing out native plants and generally wreaking havoc on intricate food webs. Invasive species compete for limited natural resources including soil, water, light, nutrients, and space. They displace native plants, replacing high-quality wildlife food sources with plants that are inedible, less nutritious, toxic, or otherwise harmful. Invasive plants draw pollinators away from native plants, hybridize with them, push rare plants closer to extinction, and reduce native biodiversity.

© Judy Fulton

Kudzu (*Pueraria montana* var. *lobata*) completely engulfing native vegetation

Ecological Impacts of Invasive Plants

- Reduce populations of native species, locally and regionally
- Form monocultures that displace native plants and alter plant communities
- Shade out native plants through dense vertical growth, or by growing over and on top of plants
- Replace native plants with non-native species that do not support native insects, which are essential food for birds and other wildlife
- Inhibit native plants through allelopathy (i.e., release of chemicals that interfere with plant growth)
- Suppress mycorrhizae, the beneficial soil fungi that help native plants take up water and minerals
- Hybridize with native plants, diluting and altering their qualities
- Kill native trees and shrubs by girdling (i.e., blocking the movement of water and nutrients through vascular tissue)
- Alter soil functions, nitrification, and pH, making conditions less favorable for native species
- Disrupt and interfere with ecological processes such as successional change from field to forest
- Alter hydrological conditions, causing degradation of native plant habitat and making conditions less favorable for native species
- Increase the frequency and intensity of wildland fires, resulting in destruction of native plant communities and further invasion by alien plant species

Invasive species spread rapidly and unabated, changing forests, meadows, wetlands and other natural plant communities into landscapes dominated by single-species monocultures with little ecological value. Invasive plants also impede recreational activities like boating, fishing, swimming, hiking, and biking by overgrowing trails and riparian areas or forming impenetrable tangles in shallow water. Once established over large areas, invasives require enormous amounts of time, labor, and money to manage, and are usually difficult if not impossible to eliminate.

How are invasive plants introduced?
Non-native plants are introduced by people intentionally and accidentally, for use as food, forage, medicine, erosion control, windbreaks, and ornamentals. Examples of some significant introductions of alien plants that have led to establishment of invasive species are listed below.

INVASIVE PLANT INTRODUCTIONS

Aquatic plants have been introduced intentionally for ornamental purposes and unintentionally when aquarium hobbyists dump unwanted plants into ponds, lakes, rivers, streams, and other waters.

Ornamentals have frequently escaped from plantings to become significant environmental weeds. According to Reichard & White 2001, the majority of invasive woody plant species in the U.S. (e.g., Chinese and Japanese wisteria, Asian bittersweet, Japanese barberry, Amur honeysuckle, princess tree, bamboos, and privets) were introduced for their horticultural value. Specifically, 192 of 235 woody plant species used in landscapes were documented to have escaped from cultivation and to be causing major ecological damage to natural habitats.

Kudzu was introduced to the U.S. from Japan in 1876 at the Philadelphia Centennial Exposition for forage and ornamental uses. From 1935 to the early 1950s, the U.S. Department of Agriculture encouraged farmers in the South to plant kudzu to reduce soil erosion, and Franklin D. Roosevelt's Civilian Conservation Corps used it widely. Kudzu was eventually recognized as a pest weed, and in 1970 the USDA removed it from the list of permissible cover plants. However, this action came too late: kudzu's out-of-control growth was widely recognized, earning it the moniker "the vine that ate the South."

Other species have arrived undetected in imported products, soil, ship ballast, packaging materials and other items. For example, Japanese stiltgrass, a widespread invasive species, was used as packing material for porcelain and likely got a start when some of the dried grass containing seed was discarded outdoors.

How do invasive plants spread?
Invasive plants spread by seeds and vegetatively via rhizomes, runners, shoots, tubers, and bulbs. Seeds and plant fragments are dispersed by people, wildlife, water, wind, and storms. People spread invasives by planting them, by using contaminated soil and horticultural materials, by legal and illegal dumping, and by carrying seeds and other plant parts on their shoes, clothing, and equipment.

Animals spread invasive plants when they consume fruits and defecate seeds in new locations, and when they inadvertently carry fruits or seeds on their fur and feet. Invasive aquatic plants not removed from boats, trailers, and other items can be transported between water bodies.

> **PREVENT SPREAD OF INVASIVE PLANTS**
> · Familiarize yourself with invasive plant species in your area.
> · Do not buy or plant invasive species; use natives instead.
> · Remove invasive plants on your property and replace them with species that are native where you live.
> · Support regulations that restrict the sale of invasive plants and require plant sellers to inform buyers of plants that are invasive.

Healthy ecosystems and ecological services

Healthy ecosystems are essential for maintaining strong, diverse populations of native animals, plants, fungi, and other organisms, and for our survival and quality of life. Our forests, wetlands, meadows, and other natural habitats provide critical ecological services, including cleaning air and water; regulating air, water and soil temperature; stabilizing soil; controlling floodwaters; and pollinating crops and native plants.

Local parks, woodlots, and residential properties can provide crucial habitat for native species. Removing non-native and invasive plants, and replacing them with locally native species will help provide essential food, hosts, and shelter for native wildlife. Where white-tailed deer (*Odocoileus virginianus*) populations exceed the carrying capacity of the land, population reduction is needed to ensure survival of native species and natural communities. We all have a role to play in helping to conserve our natural areas and biodiversity for future generations.

Native plants and local ecotypes

Choosing the best native plants for your location will be easier once you understand the ecological and environmental conditions you have. An ecotype is a genetically distinct population of a native species with unique physiological and morphological characteristics resulting from adaptation to a particular habitat and environmental conditions. If you have access to local ecotypes, you will be able to provide local fauna with the non-altered native plants they depend upon.

Non-native plants, whether invasive or not, offer little value to native wildlife and some are even harmful, for example:

- **Heavenly bamboo** (*Nandina domestica*) berries contain highly toxic hydrogen cyanide and have been confirmed as the cause of mass mortality events in cedar waxwings (Woldemeskel et al. 2010), which depend on fruit as a major component of their winter diet.

- **Autumn-olive** (*Elaeagnus umbellata*) berries lack the fat and flavonoid content of native fruits that is needed by migratory birds for their long flights to Central and South America.

Heavenly bamboo (*Nandina domestica*)

- **Garlic mustard** (*Alliaria petiolata*) is toxic to the West Virginia white, falcate orange-tip, and mustard white butterflies, whose larvae are killed by feeding on the stems and leaves.

Native plant cultivars and hybrids

Use of cultivars and hybrids of native plants could have undesirable effects on wildlife, but further research is needed. For centuries, native plants have been altered through selective breeding, producing varieties that are genetically and physically different from parent species.

These human-designed plants can be cultivars (i.e., the progeny of a single species) or hybrids (i.e., the progeny of two or more species) and vary from their wild relatives in important traits, such as leaf and stem chemistry, nectar and pollen quality, color, and other features. As a result, native insects may avoid or get reduced benefits from feeding on cultivars.

Going native may be addictive

There is an astonishing variety of attractive and hardy native herbaceous and woody plants to choose from. You may soon find yourself hooked on converting your exotic-dominated landscape into an ecological wonderland teeming with pollinators, and supporting native birds and other wildlife. The "Native Plants for Landscapes" section provides a tantalizing introduction to some of the wonderful native grasses, sedges, ferns, forbs, shrubs, trees, and vines that are available in the mid-Atlantic region.

CLIMATE CHANGE & INVASIVE PLANTS

Greenhouse gases

Human activities since the Industrial Revolution have increased atmospheric concentrations of carbon dioxide (CO_2), methane, and other gases, amplifying the Earth's natural greenhouse effect. CO_2 is called a "greenhouse gas" because it absorbs and radiates heat. Atmospheric CO_2 levels have increased dramatically over the past century as a result of human-caused CO_2 emissions. These higher CO_2 levels have led to rapid warming of Earth's air and water, causing drastic changes to global weather patterns.

ATMOSPHERIC CO_2 AMOUNTS & ANNUAL EMISSIONS (1750–2021)

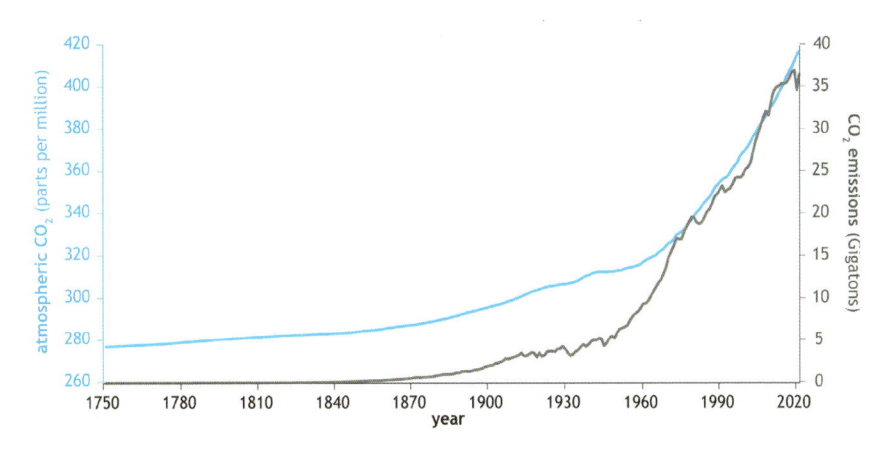

NOAA Climate.gov Data: NOAA, ETHZ, Our World in Data

Warmer temperatures have resulted in increased atmospheric moisture, heightened storm activity and intensity, more extreme precipitation patterns such as drought and flooding, more intense wildland fires, and rising sea levels. Recent and projected increases in CO_2 are likely to promote and accelerate plant growth because this molecule is the source of carbon, which plants use for photosynthesis. However, as with any resource (e.g., light, water and nutrients), not all plant species respond in the same way. Based on initial data from Lewis Ziska (2003), invasive plants may benefit more from higher CO_2 levels than native species.

CO₂ Emissions & Atmospheric Levels

- As of 2021, atmospheric CO_2 was nearing 420 ppm, up from 280 ppm in the 1800s. The current level last occurred on Earth four million years ago, a time when sea level was 78 feet higher and temperatures were 7° F warmer.
- The annual rate of increase in atmospheric CO_2 over the past 60 years was about 100 times faster than anything observed previously in Earth's history.
- The ocean has absorbed enough CO_2 to lower its pH by 0.3 units, a 30% increase in acidity.

Ecological responses to climate change

Climate change will affect native and alien plants, animals, and other organisms differently, according to each species' inherent ability to respond and adapt to rapidly changing environmental conditions. Specialized insect and plant relationships, such as host plant and pollinator associations that are tightly linked as a result of coevolution, may face particular challenges due to temporal effects on their availability. For example, if plant and pollinator ranges shift away from each other, some plant species may flower before or after their specialist pollinators have emerged, resulting in reduced seed production and genetic exchange.

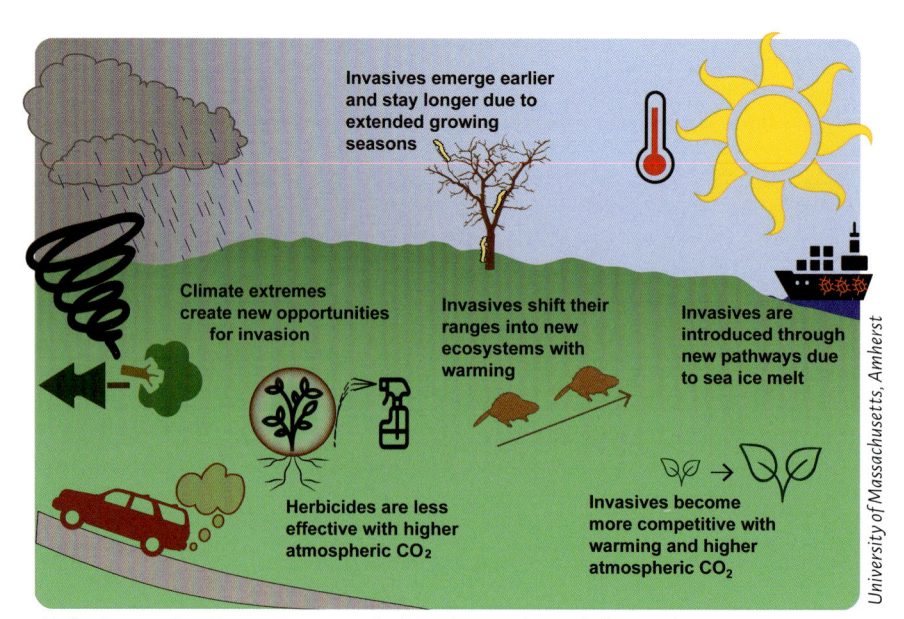

Major interactions between non-native invasive species and climate change

Invasive plants expected to fare better

Plants that are able to adapt quickly to extremes of soil saturation and drying, and that respond to warmer temperatures and higher CO_2 levels with increased growth and vigor, are expected to fare best. For example, plant physiologist Lewis Ziska (2004) found that under higher CO_2 concentrations, Canada thistle grew more vigorously and was less susceptible to currently recommended doses of the herbicide glyphosate. These changes are likely due to the plant putting more resources into the root system. This research has important implications for the future control of agricultural weeds and invasive plants spreading in natural areas. Comparative studies have consistently shown that invasive plants perform better than natives when CO_2 levels are higher and temperatures are warmer.

MID-ATLANTIC & NORTHEAST PARTICULARLY VULNERABLE

According to the Northeast Regional Invasive Species and Climate Change Network (RISCC), the Northeast and mid-Atlantic regions are particularly vulnerable to interactions between invasions and climate change because:

- Northerly latitudes are warming more than southerly latitudes, leading to more rapid environmental changes.

- Substantial urban and suburban development in the Northeast and mid-Atlantic is causing atmospheric CO_2 content to increase more rapidly compared to more rural areas, resulting in invasive plants becoming more competitive.

- The Northeast and mid-Atlantic are projected to see more extreme precipitation events, both drought and excessive rainfall, which will elevate levels of disturbance and stress on native ecosystems.

- Prevalent southerly invasive species are shifting their ranges north, making these regions hotspots for future invasion.

What you can do

For recommendations on what you can do to help reduce CO_2 and methane emissions and mitigate the effects of climate change, see the U.S. Environmental Protection Agency's "What you can do about climate change," the Natural Resources Defense Council's "How you can stop global warming," and the David Suzuki Foundation's "Top 10 things you can do about climate change."

RESTORING NATURE AT HOME

Nature is under siege from human activities including introduction of invasive species, habitat destruction, air pollution, water pollution, plastic pollution, overuse of pesticides, excessive nighttime lighting, climate change (resulting in increased warming, storm intensity, drought, soil saturation, and fires), and wanton destruction of Earth's insect life. You can take action to help turn the tide. The material in this section is based largely on information from Douglas Tallamy's book *Nature's Best Hope: A New Approach to Conservation That Starts in Your Yard*, and the website Homegrown National Park.

What can you do to help restore nature?

Love the bugs. Learn to appreciate the insects around you rather than seeing them as unwanted pests. Insects are mostly beneficial and make our world livable. As Edward O. Wilson noted, "Insects are the little things that run the world."

Lose the lawn. Reduce your lawn and restrict turf to paths and small areas. Exotic turfgrass lawns provide little ecological value and typically require irrigation, mowing, and sometimes fertilizers and pesticides. In addition to being biological wastelands dominated by single species, turfgrass density impedes critical soil access for pupating moths and butterflies.

Leave the leaves. Allowing leaves to remain in your yard, especially underneath trees, will allow caterpillars in trees and shrubs to safely reach the soil, burrow in, and pupate. Mosses and groundcovers also facilitate this process.

Pull the plug on pest plants. Remove invasive plants from your property and replace them with native plants, which will enhance the ecological value of your yard and reduce the spread of invasives.

Set aside the pesticides. Avoid using herbicides and insecticides or, when needed, use them minimally and judiciously. Sometimes herbicides are necessary to effectively kill persistent invasive plants, including their roots, with minimal soil disturbance. However, pesticides can harm or kill beneficial insects (e.g., bees, lacewings, and lady beetles) and desirable plants.

Scrap the zap trap. Millions of bug zappers are sold each year to unknowing people who believe the advertising that the traps actually kill large numbers of mosquitoes. In fact, studies have shown that nothing could be further from the truth; mosquitoes are attracted to our exhaled carbon dioxide, sweat, and body heat. Every year, bug zappers kill billions of beneficial insects including moths, lacewings, aquatic insects, and beetles. The traps are eliminating the essential insect fauna that serves as our life support system, while rarely catching mosquitoes! Similarly, mosquito control companies that regularly spray your yard are killing large numbers of beneficial insects and failing to slow mosquito reproduction. Save your money and protect beneficial species.

Make a mosquito trap. Get a bucket and add some water, grass clippings, and a mosquito "dunk." Dunks are made of a naturally occurring soil bacterium called *Bacillus thuringiensis* ssp. *israelensis* (Bti) that, according to the U.S. EPA, kills only mosquito, black fly, and fungus gnat larvae. Every 3–4 weeks, empty the bucket and make a fresh trap. Also, drain all standing water in your yard every few days and wear insect-repellent, long-sleeved shirts and pants to keep mosquitoes away.

Be pro-wildlife. Make your environment safe for wildlife: cover basement window wells, cap chimney flues, add wildlife escape ramps in garden pools, and keep cats indoors (they kill millions of birds and other animals each year). Install ground-directed, motion-activated outdoor lights to avoid attracting and killing moths, beetles, aquatic insects, and other beneficial species. This type of lighting is best for safety, wildlife and the environment. The International Dark-Sky Association is a great resource for the best outdoor light fixtures.

White-eyed vireo parents depend on caterpillars from native plants like oaks, cherries and sycamores to rear young

When they go low, you mow high. Set your mower blade to 3" or higher. It has been demonstrated over many decades of research that maintaining higher turf helps prevent weeds, keeps lawns healthier, and reduces polluted runoff into waterways. Taller grass also protects vertebrates and invertebrates moving through turf from being injured or killed.

Cater to the caterpillars. Use native host plants that support the insect larvae required by birds and other wildlife to successfully rear their young. In the process, you will be attracting beautiful native moths and butterflies to your property, including silk moths, sphinx moths, monarch butterflies, hummingbird clearwings, tiger and zebra swallowtail butterflies, and many other species.

Plant with abandon. Native insects are crucial to the global food web that keeps us alive. For the biggest impact, incorporate lots of different kinds of native plants in your landscapes.

Bee specific. Many indigenous bees are specialists, requiring pollen from particular native plant genera to rear their larvae. According to Sam Droege (USGS Bee Inventory & Monitoring Lab, personal communication), about 500 species of bees native to the Mid-Atlantic region are highly specialized, and feed their young pollen from just a few native plant species. In almost all cases, non-native plants are not acceptable replacements. These specialist bees are uncommon and of particular conservation concern.

Keystone plants are the key. Plants like oaks, wild cherries, and willows are referred to as "keystone" species because they host hundreds of species of moths and butterflies, more than other genera. Without them, the entire natural community is at risk of collapse. Many alien and cultivated versions of native plants are available, but they lack the unique chemistries and nutritional qualities of native species. Be sure to incorporate keystone species into your plantings.

Common eastern bumble bee (*Bombus impatiens*) on New England aster (*Symphyotrichum novae-angliae*)

Maria Cristina Niciporciukas

Home sweet home. Be part of the Homegrown National Park initiative. Check out the HNP website to learn how to qualify and register your property.

Nudge your neighbors. Networking with your neighbors is a great way to enlarge the area of a Homegrown National Park. It is also a good way to share plants and knowledge. Talk with your town officials and homeowners association. Lobby for ordinances that encourage landscapes dominated by native perennial forbs, grasses, and woody plants.

Selecting native plants

Native plants are the basis of complex food webs associated with ecosystems. They are adapted to certain soil types, soil moisture levels, sun exposures, ambient temperatures, and other environmental conditions. Native plant species have traits that have developed over thousands of years of coevolution with other organisms and the environment. As a result of long-term evolution and natural selection, most herbivorous insects have become specialized on certain plant families, genera, and sometimes even species: they depend upon these plant taxa for survival. To provide the best plants for native fauna, choose species native to the physiographic province and ecoregion where you live.

Keystone Native Plants—Examples

Grasses. Broomsedge (*Andropogon virginicus*), little bluestem (*Schizachyrium scoparium*), bottlebrush grass (*Elymus hystrix*), panicgrasses (*Dichanthelium* and *Panicum*), purpletop (*Tridens flavus*)

Sedges and rushes. Pennsylvania sedge (*Carex pensylvanica*), fox sedge (*Carex vulpinoidea*), common rush (*Juncus effusus*), hedgehog woodrush (*Luzula echinata*), woolgrass (*Scirpus cyperinus*)

Forbs (spring). Spring beauty (*Claytonia virginica*), bloodroot (*Sanguinaria canadensis*), wild ginger (*Asarum canadense*), mayapple (*Podophyllum peltatum*), twinleaf (*Jeffersonia diphylla*), red trillium (*Trillium erectum*), yellow trout lily (*Erythronium americanum*), golden ragwort (*Packera aurea*), wild strawberry (*Fragaria virginiana*), wild blue phlox (*Phlox divaricata*), Virginia bluebells (*Mertensia virginica*), wild columbine (*Aquilegia canadensis*)

Forbs (summer). Swamp milkweed (*Asclepias incarnata*), Maryland tick-trefoil (*Desmodium marilandicum*), white wood aster (*Eurybia divaricata*), woodland sunflower (*Helianthus divaricatus*), striped cream violet (*Viola striata*), cutleaf coneflower (*Rudbeckia laciniata*), spotted beebalm (*Monarda punctata*), wreath goldenrod (*Solidago caesia*), late purple aster (*Symphyotrichum patens*)

Shrubs. Highbush blueberry (*Vaccinium corymbosum*), silky dogwood (*Cornus amomum*), fringetree (*Chionanthus virginicus*), mountain laurel (*Kalmia latifolia*), New Jersey tea (*Ceanothus americanus*), spicebush (*Lindera benzoin*), mapleleaf viburnum (*Viburnum acerifolium*), buttonbush (*Cephalanthus occidentalis*), downy serviceberry (*Amelanchier arborea*), witch hazel (*Hamamelis virginiana*)

Trees. River birch (*Betula nigra*), black cherry (*Prunus serotina*), eastern cottonwood (*Populus deltoides*), white oak (*Quercus alba*), willow oak (*Quercus phellos*), black willow (*Salix nigra*), pawpaw (*Asimina triloba*), sassafras (*Sassafras albidum*), sweetgum (*Liquidambar styraciflua*), Eastern redbud (*Cercis canadensis*), southern hackberry (*Celtis laevigata*), American elm (*Ulmus americana*), slippery elm (*Ulmus rubra*)

Vines. Coral honeysuckle (*Lonicera sempervirens*), moonseed (*Menispermum canadense*), yellow passionflower (*Passiflora lutea*), trumpet creeper (*Campsis radicans*), Virgin's-bower (*Clematis virginiana*), Virginia creeper (*Parthenocissus quinquefolia*), American wisteria (*Wisteria frutescens*), white-leaf greenbriar (*Smilax glauca*), fox grape (*Vitis vulpina*)

PHYSIOGRAPHIC PROVINCES & ECOREGIONS

Physiographic Provinces

A physiographic province is a large-scale geographic region with a characteristic geomorphology (i.e., "earth form") that has been affected by climate and geologic factors acting over millennia to form unique landscapes with specific topographical and physical characteristics. From west to east, the five major physiographic provinces in the mid-Atlantic region are: Appalachian Plateaus, Ridge and Valley, Blue Ridge, Piedmont, and Coastal Plain. A finger of the New England province covers small portions of northern New Jersey and eastern Pennsylvania. These five major provinces encompass the fourteen finer-scale mid-Atlantic ecoregions described and illustrated below.

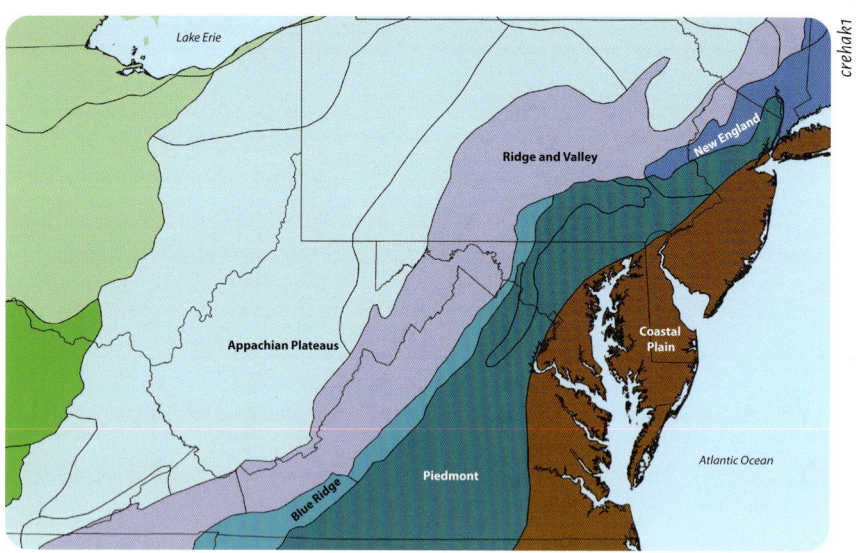

U.S. Physiographic Provinces (USGS 2021)

Ecoregions

Ecoregions are areas defined by ecological similarities and environmental resources. The ecoregion concept was developed by Omernik in 1987 and mapped in collaboration with the U.S. EPA, other federal agencies, state resource management agencies, and Canadian and Mexican experts. Ecoregions reflect geographic areas with similar abiotic, biotic, aquatic, and terrestrial ecosystem components, and include humans as part of the biota. More specifically, these components include underlying geology, surface landforms, soils, hydrology, climate, vegetation, and wildlife. The purpose of designating ecoregions was to provide a foundation for detailed ecosystem monitoring, assessment, and research. Ecoregions were intended to facilitate implementation of consistent ecosystem management strategies by government and non-governmental organizations in areas where resources and responsibilities overlap.

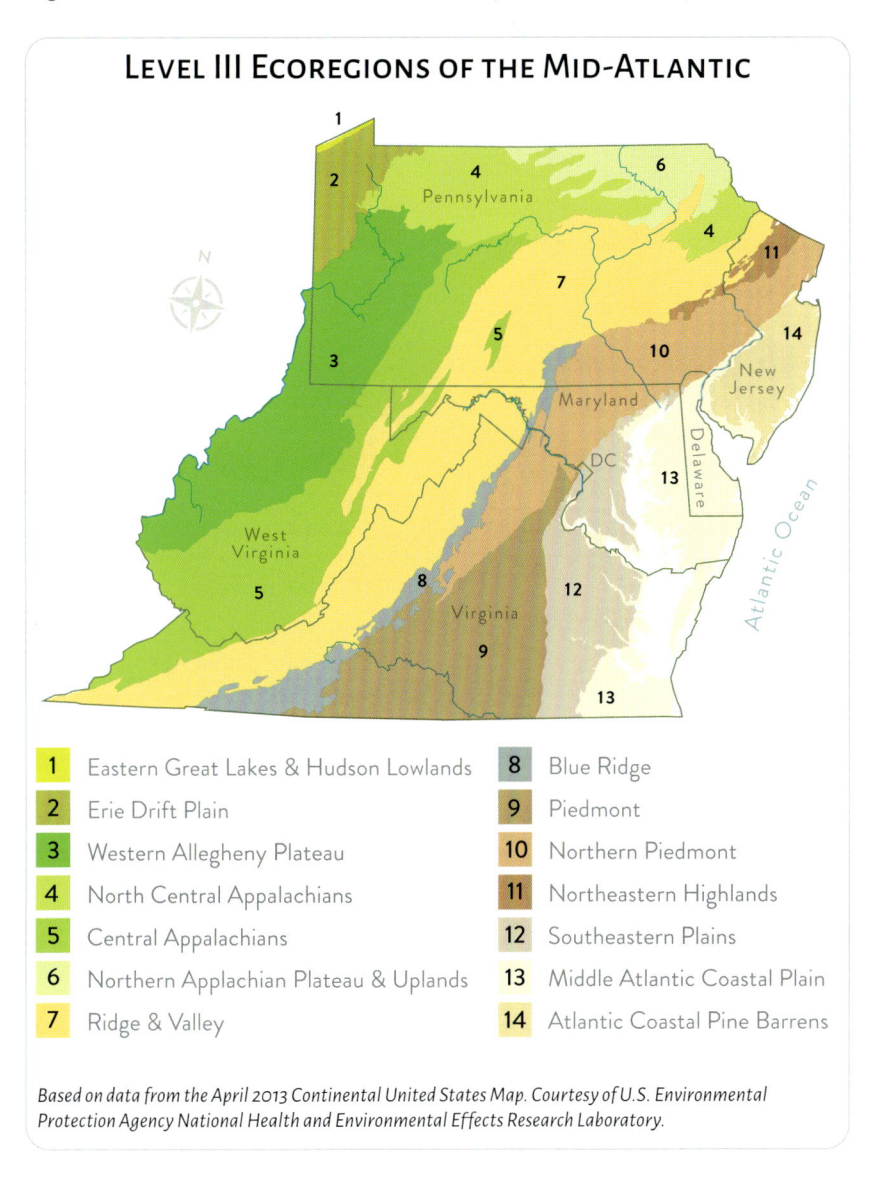

LEVEL III ECOREGIONS OF THE MID-ATLANTIC

1	Eastern Great Lakes & Hudson Lowlands	8	Blue Ridge
2	Erie Drift Plain	9	Piedmont
3	Western Allegheny Plateau	10	Northern Piedmont
4	North Central Appalachians	11	Northeastern Highlands
5	Central Appalachians	12	Southeastern Plains
6	Northern Applachian Plateau & Uplands	13	Middle Atlantic Coastal Plain
7	Ridge & Valley	14	Atlantic Coastal Pine Barrens

Based on data from the April 2013 Continental United States Map. Courtesy of U.S. Environmental Protection Agency National Health and Environmental Effects Research Laboratory.

Find Your Ecoregion. Knowing what ecoregion you live in will help you decide which native plants are the most appropriate for your location. To determine your ecoregion, use the map tab at NatureServe's *LandScope America*.

INVASIVE PLANT SUMMARIES

This section provides detailed summaries on 81 plant species (6 aquatic plants, 11 grasses—including 4 bamboos, 1 sedge, 20 forbs, 19 shrubs, 8 trees and 16 vines) that have been reported by botanists, ecologists, wildlife biologists, land managers and other experts to be invasive in mid-Atlantic natural areas. While these plants represent some of the worst invaders in our area, there are hundreds more, with new invasive species discovered every year.

Each plant summary includes the following information from the sources listed:

- ***Taxonomic nomenclature (scientific name) and native origin.*** USDA Agricultural Research Service Germplasm Resources Information Network (GRIN) website
- ***Background on species introduction.*** Various printed and online sources
- ***Distribution.*** Floras, USGS Non-indigenous Aquatic Species (NAS), University of Georgia Early Detection and Distribution Mapping System (EDDMapS)
- ***Habitat.*** Floras, online sources, experts
- ***Ecological threat.*** Publications, online sources, experts, personal experience
- ***Plant description, biology, and method of spread.*** Floras, online sources, experts, personal experience
- ***Look-alikes.*** Suggestions of the authors, other sources
- ***Prevention & control.*** Invasive species publications, online sources, experts, personal experience
- ***Native alternatives.*** Publications, online sources, experts, personal experience

The **Other Invasive Plants** section includes 11 additional species that, while not currently widespread in the mid-Atlantic region, are of concern due to their invasive tendencies. They include: goutweed (*Aegopodium podagraria*), broadleaf helleborine (*Epipactis helleborine*), giant hogweed (*Heracleum mantegazzianum*), Spanish bluebells (*Hyacinthoides hispanica*), yellow archangel (*Lamium galeobdolon*), summer snowflake (*Leucojum aestivum*), butterflybush (*Buddleja davidii*), castor-aralia (*Kalopanax septemlobus*), jetbead (*Rhodotypos scandens*), Amur corktree (*Phellodendron amurense*) and Chinese yam (*Dioscorea polystachya*).

Report invasive species using EDDMapS (eddmaps.org) and/or iNaturalist, and remove them from natural areas to prevent their establishment and spread.

Floral Distancing

Important characteristics of flowering plants used for differentiating plant taxa include completeness of flowers, presence or absence of male and female organs, and location of flowers on the same plant or separate plants. These plant sexuality features are explained and illustrated below.

PLANT SEXUALITY

Complete flower. A flower that has all four main parts: *sepals, petals, stamens,* and *pistils (carpels).*

Incomplete flower. A flower lacking one or more parts of a complete flower.

Perfect, bisexual or hermaphroditic flower. A flower with *both* staminate (male) and pistillate/carpellate (female) structures. Most flowering plants have perfect flowers.

Imperfect or unisexual flower. A flower that has *only one functional sex*. Plant taxa with imperfect flowers are either *monoecious, dioecious,* or a variation on this theme. Many taxa, such as hackberry (*Celtis*) have both unisexual and bisexual flowers on the same plant.

Monoecious **("one house").** *Separate* male and female flowers are found *on the same plant*. Examples: All oaks (*Quercus*) and most cucurbits (*Cucurbita*).

Dioecious **("two houses").** *Separate* male and female flowers are found on *different plants*. Examples: Most hollies (*Ilex*) and most willows (*Salix*).

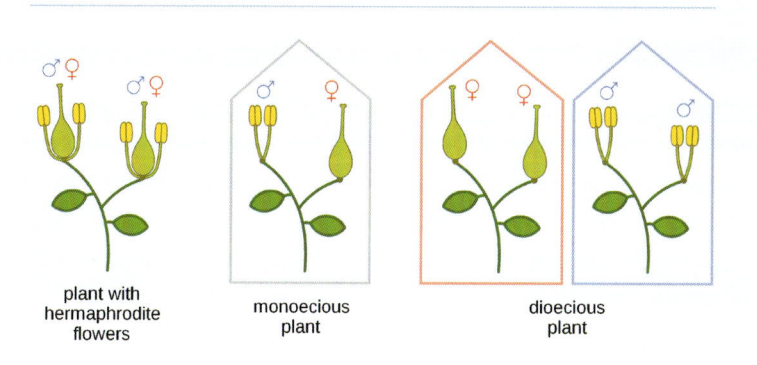

plant with hermaphrodite flowers | monoecious plant | dioecious plant

Illustration: Nefronus, CC BY-SA 4.0, commons.wikimedia.org/w/index.php?curid=80317707

AQUATIC INVASIVE PLANTS

Preventing the introduction and initial spread of aquatic invaders is the most effective and proactive approach and avoids costly control measures needed once species become established. Aquatic plants are fully adapted to an aquatic existence—either *floating freely* on the water surface or *rooted*—with a portion of the plant *just reaching, floating on,* or *extending above* the water surface. Species that complete their entire life cycle under water are referred to as **submerged aquatic vegetation** or SAV.

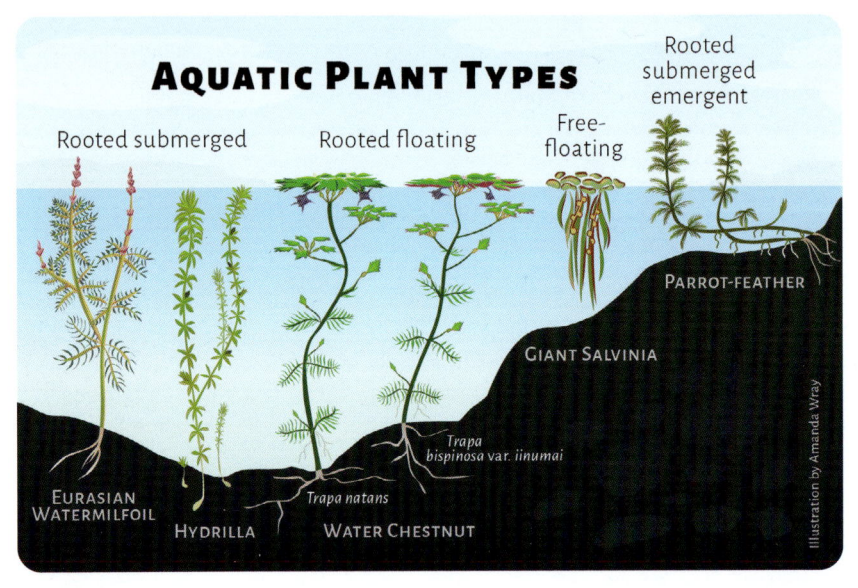

AQUATIC PLANT TYPES

Rooted submerged · Rooted floating · Free-floating · Rooted submerged emergent

Parrot-feather
Giant Salvinia
Eurasian Watermilfoil
Hydrilla
Trapa bispinosa var. *iinumai*
Trapa natans
Water Chestnut

Illustration by Amanda Wray

- **Free-floating.** Unrooted, with most of the plant on the water surface (e.g., duckweed, water hyacinth, giant salvinia).
- **Rooted floating.** Rooted, occupying the entire water column, with some of the plant on the surface (e.g., water lily, spatterdock, water chestnut).
- **Rooted submerged.** Rooted, occupying the entire water column with most of the plant just reaching the water surface (e.g., eelgrass, hydrilla, Eurasian watermilfoil).
- **Rooted submerged emergent.** Rooted with some portion of leaves and stems extending out of the water (e.g., parrot-feather, cattail).

In the tidal waters of the Chesapeake Bay watershed, resource managers usually protect all submerged aquatic vegetation (SAV), including invasive hydrilla and Eurasian watermilfoil, because these plants provide water quality benefits and habitat for macroinvertebrates, fish, shellfish, and waterfowl. In contrast to estuarine waters of the Bay, if a non-native SAV is found in a lake or enclosed water body, managers might try to eradicate it. However, if it is found in Chesapeake Bay tributaries, managers provide it the same level of protection as any SAV. Report sightings to the U.S. Geological Survey (USGS) Nonindigenous Aquatic Species database (NAS) and contact the appropriate local natural resource management agency in your state for assistance.

HYDRILLA

Hydrilla verticillata (L. f.) Royle / Frog-bit family (Hydrocharitaceae)

Robert Vidéki, bugwood.org *Robert Vidéki, bugwood.org*

Origin—Africa, Asia, Australasia, Europe

Background—Hydrilla, also known as water thyme, was first discovered in a canal in Tampa, Florida in 1952. Imported by the aquarium trade, its presence on the Delmarva Peninsula was confirmed in 1981. Hydrilla attracted national attention when infestations were found in the Potomac River in the District of Columbia in the early 1980s. According to Tippery et al. 2020, there have been at least three introductions to the U.S., with the third hydrilla strain found as recently as 2016 in the Connecticut River. The plant's name comes from Hydra, the many-headed serpent of Greek mythology that was able to regenerate after being beheaded. Hydrilla is a federally designated noxious weed.

Distribution & Habitat—Hydrilla occurs from Wisconsin to Texas and Maine to Florida, as well as in Arizona, California, Idaho, and Washington. Invaded habitats include rivers, lakes, marshes, springs and ditches with flowing or stagnant, fresh to mildly saline water of variable pH (although it does best under neutral pH conditions). Hydrilla can grow under extremely low light conditions and in water from a few inches to 50' deep.

Ecological Threat—Hydrilla outcompetes native submerged aquatic vegetation and can quickly fill a pond, a lake, or a tidal tributary of the Chesapeake Bay. In the Mid-Atlantic and Northeast, most hydrilla populations are monoecious, with both male and female flowers on the same plant. A dioecious (separate male and female plants) form with only female flowers occurs in some parts of the U.S. Fish kills can occur when dense dioecious hydrilla populations become infected by a toxic cyanobacterium. Birds and reptiles consuming these infected plants, and predators feeding on these herbivores, can be killed or impaired.

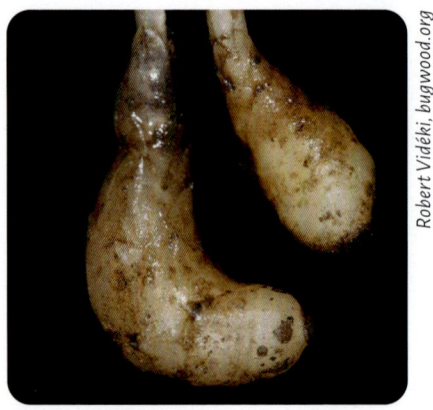

Hydrilla tubers

DESCRIPTION & BIOLOGY

Plant. Perennial rooted submerged aquatic plant. Long stems branch at the surface, grow horizontally, and form dense mats or canopies. Both the monoecious and dioecious forms of hydrilla propagate through *non-dormant* stolons and stem fragments, and through perennating structures (turions and tubers) that become detached and remain dormant in the mud for up to one year (turions) or four years (tubers). *Seeds* are a minor means of reproduction. *Turions* are dark green auxiliary winter buds about ⅛–½" long, formed in leaf axils, and covered by pointed-tipped bracts. There is evidence that turions can survive herbicide applications as well as ingestion and regurgitation by waterfowl. *Tubers* are dull white to yellowish potato-like structures, about ⅙–½" long (usually larger than turions) and attached to the creeping rhizome (root-like stem). Formed at the end of the growing season, tubers contain nutritional resources that enable hydrilla to overwinter and serve as food for waterfowl. Found up to a foot deep in mud, tubers can remain viable after several days out of the water.

Leaves. Narrow, serrated, pointed-tipped, about ⅝" long, in whorls of 3–8.

Flowers, fruits & seeds. Single, small white flowers; flower parts in threes. In North America, hydrilla is either dioecious (separate male and female plants) or monoecious (male and female flowers on the same plant). Individual female flowers—containing the ovules—are raised from the leaf axils toward the water surface on an elongated, thread-like stalk. Short-stalked male flowers emerge as buds from the leaf axils, detach and float to the water surface, where they release pollen.

AQUATIC PLANTS

Method of spread. The primary method of reproduction and spread of hydrilla in the U.S. is through *fragmentation*—the propagation of clonal plants from stem nodes; spread by seed is insignificant in comparison. Hydrilla can also be spread by stem fragments, stolons, turions, and tubers carried in or on boat livewell tanks, motors, trailers, bait pails, and other items. Boats moving through hydrilla patches shred plants, resulting in huge quantities of fragments that can move throughout a water body. New infestations can start from release of aquarium contents into ponds, lakes or other water bodies and use of hydrilla-contaminated plants for water gardens.

Look-alikes. Native common waterweed (*Elodea canadensis*) with leaves in whorls of three and no, or barely visible, serrated edges or spines; and non-native invasive Brazilian waterweed (*Egeria densa*) that generally has longer leaves and much larger flowers (up to ¾" wide) than either hydrilla or common waterweed. Both look-alikes lack tubers and turions.

Prevention & Control—Possession, sale, or transport of hydrilla is prohibited by U.S. law. Do not purchase or release hydrilla or any aquatic plant into natural waters (i.e., all flowing and still water). Contact the natural resource management agency in your state for assistance and permits prior to taking any action regarding control of aquatic vegetation.

Native Alternatives—Contact the natural resource management agency in your state for assistance and permits prior to taking any action regarding planting of aquatic vegetation.

PARROT-FEATHER

Myriophyllum aquaticum (Vell.) Verdc. / Watermilfoil family (Haloragaceae)

Leslie Mehrhoff, bugwood.org

Graves Lovell, bugwood.org

Origin—South America

Background—Parrot-feather was introduced to the U.S. as an ornamental around 1890 near the District of Columbia. It is the only dioecious (male and female flowers on separate plants) species of *Myriophyllum* in the U.S. Sold for aquatic gardens and aquariums, it has escaped to infest ponds and calm water bodies.

Distribution & Habitat—Parrot-feather has been introduced in at least 39 states in the U.S., from Minnesota to Texas and Connecticut to Florida, and in Washington, Idaho, and New Mexico. It was discovered in Utah for the first time in 2020. Parrot-feather grows in non-tidal, freshwater, and slow-moving water bodies including ponds, lakes, canals, and tributaries, and does best in high-nutrient and slightly alkaline environments.

Ecological Threat—Parrot-feather can form dense mats and compete with native aquatic plants, especially in shallow ponds, where it provides habitat for mosquito larvae.

DESCRIPTION & BIOLOGY

Plant. Perennial rooted submerged emergent aquatic plant. In the U.S., *only female plants* are found and thus are functionally sterile. Rhizomes function as a support structure for adventitious roots and provide buoyancy for emergent growth during the summer. Stolons serve as a means of dispersal, food storage, and perennation (the ability of parrot-feather to survive from one germinating season to another, especially under unfavorable conditions such as drought or winter). When submerged shoots reach the water surface, they grow with extensive branching from nodes, followed by vertical growth of emergent stems.

Leaves. Two forms: *emergent* leaves are whorled, feather-like, grayish-green, and can extend 12" above the water surface; *submerged* leaves are filamentous, pectinate, about ½–1½" long, and occur in whorls of 4–6 leaves from each node.

Flowers, fruits & seeds. Small white female flowers, about $\frac{1}{16}$" long, occur in the leaf axils on the emergent shoots; male flowers do not occur in the U.S.

Method of spread. Plant fragments are carried in or on items including boat livewells, motors, trailers, tires, fishing gear, bait buckets, and animal fur, and introduced to water bodies through dumping of aquarium contents.

Look-alikes. Native northern watermilfoil (*Myriophyllum sibiricum*), American featherfoil (*Hottonia inflata*) and water violet (*Hottonia palustris*); non-native and invasive Eurasian watermilfoil (*Myriophyllum spicatum*).

Prevention & Control—Do not release parrot-feather or any aquatic plant into natural waters (i.e., all flowing and still waters). Contact the appropriate local natural resource management agency in your state for assistance and permits prior to taking any action regarding control of aquatic vegetation.

Native Alternatives—Contact the natural resource management agency in your state for assistance and permits prior to taking any action regarding planting of aquatic vegetation.

EURASIAN WATERMILFOIL

Myriophyllum spicatum L. / Watermilfoil family (Haloragaceae)

Leslie Mehrhoff, bugwood.org

Graves Lovell, bugwood.org

Origin—Europe, Asia, North Africa

Background—Eurasian watermilfoil was introduced sometime during the late 1800s and again in 1940.

Distribution & Habitat—Eurasian watermilfoil occurs in all states in the Lower 48 except for Wyoming. In the mid-Atlantic, it is abundant in the Chesapeake Bay and tidal Potomac River. Typical habitat includes fresh to brackish water in ponds, lakes, slow-moving streams, reservoirs, estuaries, and canals. Eurasian watermilfoil is tolerant of polluted water.

Ecological Threat—Eurasian watermilfoil thrives in disturbed areas and does not typically spread into undisturbed areas where native plants are well established. It can form large, floating mats of vegetation on the surface of lakes, rivers, and other water bodies; these mats reduce light for native aquatic species. Hybridization is documented between native *M. sibiricum* and *M. spicatum*, creating a more aggressive strain with morphology from both species.

DESCRIPTION & BIOLOGY

Plant. Perennial, rooted, submerged aquatic plant with thin, green, brown to pinkish-white stems, growing to 6' long and thinning progressively further from the main stem. Axillary buds grow throughout the year.

Leaves. Bright green, typically feather-like, deeply dissected leaves in a whorl of four leaves around the stem, with 14 or more uniform-diameter leaflets on each leaf, giving the plant a delicate feathery appearance.

Flowers, fruits & seeds. Flowers are small, yellow, four-parted, and rising 2–4" above the water surface from a terminal spike. Male and female flowers can be found on the same inflorescence, each subtended by a reduced or inconspicuous bract. The stem below the inflorescence is about twice as thick as the lower stem and curved—enabling the lower stem to run parallel to the water surface. Self-fertilization occurs despite female flowers maturing before the male flowers. Fruits are dry, split open to release single seeds that can remain afloat for a day, and are eagerly ingested by waterfowl.

Method of spread. Spread is by plant fragments, rhizomes, and axillary buds attached to boat motors, trailers, tires, fishing gear, bait buckets, and animal fur, and by dumped aquarium contents. Although seeds are usually viable, they are not an important means of dispersal.

Look-alikes. Native northern watermilfoil (*Myriophyllum sibiricum*), coontail (*Ceratophyllum demersum*), and water marigold (*Megalodonta beckii*); non-native invasive parrot-feather (*Myriophyllum aquaticum*).

Prevention & Control—Do not release Eurasian watermilfoil or any aquatic plant into natural waters (i.e., all flowing and still waters). Contact the appropriate local natural resource management agency in your state for assistance and permits prior to taking any action regarding control of aquatic vegetation.

Native Alternatives—Contact the natural resource management agency in your state for assistance and permits prior to taking any action regarding planting of aquatic vegetation.

GIANT SALVINIA

Salvinia molesta D.S. Mitch. / Floating fern family (Salviniaceae)

Origin—South America

Background—Giant salvinia, also known as water fern or kariba-weed, is an *aquatic fern* that was introduced for its ornamental interest. Widely planted in

Robert Vidéki, bugwood.org

Leslie Mehrhoff, bugwood.org

arboreta and garden pools, it first escaped cultivation to natural water bodies in the U.S. in 1998.

Distribution & Habitat—Giant salvinia populations are found from Texas to North Carolina, and California, Nevada, Puerto Rico, and the Hawaiian Islands. In 2000, a small population was discovered in ornamental ponds in the District of Columbia, but was quickly eradicated.

Ecological Threat—Giant salvinia poses a serious threat to lakes, ponds, streams, rivers, other freshwater wetlands, and cultivated rice fields. It grows rapidly and spreads across water surfaces, forming dense floating mats that cut off light to other aquatic plants, reduce oxygen content, and degrade water quality for fish and other aquatic organisms.

DESCRIPTION & BIOLOGY

Plant. Free-floating aquatic fern with leaves that become compressed into chains in older plants.

Leaves. About ½–1½" long, oval, folded; upper leaf surfaces are covered with arching hairs (trichomes) that look like "egg beaters."

Flowers, fruits & seeds. Giant salvinia is a fern, not a flowering plant, and produces spores. However, in the U.S. it typically does not produce viable spores and is thus functionally sterile.

Method of spread. Spread is by dumping of aquarium contents and by plant fragments carried on wildlife, boats, fishing gear, boots and other items.

Look-alikes. Other non-native *Salvinia* species.

Prevention & Control—Possession, sale, or transport of giant salvinia is prohibited by U.S. law. Do not purchase or release giant salvinia or any aquatic plant into natural waters (i.e., all flowing and still water). Contact the appropriate local natural resource management agency in your state for assistance and permits prior to taking any action regarding control of aquatic vegetation.

Mic Julien, bugwood.org

Native Alternatives—Contact the natural resource management agency in your state for assistance and permits prior to taking any action regarding planting of aquatic vegetation.

WATER CHESTNUT

Two-horned Water Chestnut (*Trapa bispinosa* Roxb. var. *iinumai* Nakano) / Eurasian Water Chestnut (*Trapa natans* L.) / Water chestnut family (Trapaceae)

Blythe Merritt

Origin—**Two-horned:** China, Korea, Japan; **Eurasian:** Europe, Asia, Africa

Background—Eurasian water chestnut, also known as bullnut, water nut, water caltrop, and horned water chestnut, was first introduced to the U.S. in Massachusetts around 1874; its fruits have four spines, or horns. A new species of water chestnut was discovered in Virginia in 2014 and is the first report of this species in the U.S. Researchers eventually identified it as *Trapa bispinosa* var. *iinumai*, known as two-horned water chestnut, two-spined water chestnut, and two-horned *Trapa*.

Distribution & Habitat—Eurasian water chestnut is found throughout the mid-Atlantic and northeastern U.S. from Delaware and Maryland to New Hampshire. As of July 2022, two-horned water chestnut has been found in Virginia and Maryland, and it could easily be dispersed to adjacent states. Both species grow in freshwater intertidal areas to 12' deep and prefer nutrient-rich lakes and rivers.

Ecological Threat—Water chestnut forms dense floating mats that severely limit the ability of light to reach the photosynthesizing aquatic organisms that form the basis of water ecosystems. These mats can also reduce oxygen levels to significant depths, resulting in increased potential for fish kills. Water chestnut infestations compete with native aquatic vegetation.

DESCRIPTION & BIOLOGY

Plant. Annual rooted floating aquatic plant with fine roots that anchor plants in the mud and submerged stems that can grow 12–15' long. A single seed produces a plant with multiple stems that branch to produce numerous terminal floating rosettes of leaves. Flowers and fruits are borne in leaf axils of the rosette.

Leaves. Two forms: *floating* leaves in rosettes at the water surface are quadrangular with saw-tooth margins and an inflated leaf stalk that provides buoyancy for the leaf blades; *submerged* leaves are finely divided and look like roots. Leaf undersides are green (*Tn*) or dark red (*Tbi*).

Flowers, fruits & seeds. Flowering occurs from June through November or until the first hard freeze. Flowers have 4 white petals, 4 green sepals, and 4 stamens (*Tn*) or 4 pink petals, 4 pink sepals, and 4–6 stamens (*Tbi*). The fruit has a fleshy green, mottled outer skin that sloughs off to reveal a hard, black, nut-like seed with four (*Tn*) or two (*Tbi*) spines. Seeds are 1–2" across. Germination occurs in spring when water temperatures reach about 50°F.

Method of spread. Spread is by rosettes that break free and by barbed seeds clinging to waterfowl feathers, mammal fur, clothing, nets, wooden boats, construction equipment, and other items.

Look-alikes. Non-native mosaic flower (*Ludwigia sedioides*).

Prevention & Control—Do not release water chestnut or any aquatic plant into natural waters (i.e., all flowing and still water). Contact the appropriate local natural resource management agency in your state for assistance and permits prior to taking any action regarding control of aquatic vegetation.

Native Alternatives—Contact the natural resource management agency in your state for assistance and permits prior to taking any action regarding planting of aquatic vegetation.

TRAPA LEAVES, FLOWERS AND FRUITS

Trapa natans

Leaf: underside green

Flower: white petals, green sepals, 4 stamens

Fruit and seed: 4-spined (*seed shown*)

Trapa bispinosa var. *iinumai*

Leaf: underside dark red

Flower: pink petals, pink sepals, 4–6 stamens

Fruit and seed: 2-spined (*fruit shown*)

All photos this page by Lynde Dodd, USACE-ERDC

EURASIAN VS. TWO-HORNED WATER CHESTNUT

AQUATIC PLANTS

Trapa natans
Eurasian water chestnut

Trapa bispinosa var. iinumai
Two-horned water chestnut

A. **Leaf undersides:** *Tn*-green; *Tbi*-dark red
B. **Flowers:** *Tn*-white petals, green sepals, 4 stamens
   Tbi-pink petals, red sepals, 6 stamens
C. **Fruit:** Green; *Tn*-4 spines; *Tbi*-2 spines
D. **Seed:** Black; *Tn*-4 spines; *Tbi*-2 spines

This illustration is licensed under a Creative Commons Attribution-No Derivatives 4.0 International License and was created by Amanda Katherine Wray (amandawray.com)

TERRESTRIAL INVASIVE PLANTS

Ecological and Environmental Effects of Invasive Plants

The ecological and environmental effects of invasive plants vary by habit (e.g., forb, tree or vine). Impacts include displacing native plants by utilizing growing space, water, sunlight, and soil nutrients; producing extensive underground root systems that impede native plants; weakening and killing native plants by covering and girdling them; releasing allelopathic chemicals that inhibit growth of plants and soil mycorrhizae; changing soil pH and nitrification rate; modifying hydrological conditions; and altering natural fire regimes.

Effects of Invasive Plants by Habit—Examples

HERBACEOUS PLANTS Invasive grasses, sedges, rushes, and forbs are low-growing and affect the environment from the ground level to about 6'.

- **Garlic mustard** (*Alliaria petiolata*) is a biennial forb that produces large, robust flowering plants in the spring of its second year, releases allelopathic chemicals and forms extensive monocultures that push out and exclude native spring-flowering species.
- **Japanese stiltgrass** (*Microstegium vimineum*) is an annual grass that emerges in late spring and grows through the summer, increasing in height and width and forming dense patches that displace and exclude native plants.

SHRUBS Invasive shrub impacts extend from the ground to about 15–20' high. These plants create dense shade and displace native herbaceous plants and seedlings of woody plants.

- **Amur honeysuckle** (*Lonicera maackii*) and **Morrow's honeysuckle** (*Lonicera morrowii*) form extensive, dense thickets that exclude native plants and adversely affect the nesting success of some native bird species.
- **Japanese barberry** (*Berberis thunbergii*) increases soil pH, making conditions unsuitable for many native plants that prefer acidic soils; and creates shady, humid conditions that are favorable to the black-legged tick (*Ixodes scapularis*), carrier of *Borrelia burgdorferi*, the bacterium that causes Lyme disease.

TREES Impacts of invasive trees extend from the ground to the forest mid-story or canopy level.

- **Norway maple** (*Acer platanoides*) and **paper mulberry** (*Broussonetia papyrifera*) create dense stands of deep shade, making conditions unfavorable for native plants and inhibiting plant community development.

- **Tree-of-heaven** (*Ailanthus altissimus*) releases allelopathic chemicals that inhibit the growth of native plants. It also serves as the primary host for the invasive spotted lanternfly (*Lycorma delicatula*).

VINES Invasive vines affect native plants and habitats at all levels, from the ground to the forest canopy. Because vines grow from their tips, their snake-like growth enables them to cover large areas rapidly. According to Matthews et al. (2016), non-native vines are most prevalent near forest edges; vines in the crowns of trees reduce tree growth and tree survivorship, especially near forest edges. The proportion of trees with non-native vines is increasing and is likely to result in long-term changes in forest structure, composition, and process through increased tree mortality. Over time, the effects of non-native, tree-climbing vines could result in further shrinking of remnant forest patches and pose an increasing threat to small urban forests.

- **Porcelainberry** (*Ampelopsis glandulosa* var. *brevipedunculata*), **sweet autumn clematis** (*Clematis terniflora*), **Asian bittersweet** (*Celastrus orbiculatus*), and **mile-a-minute** (*Persicaria perfoliata*) grow vigorously over herbaceous plants, shrubs and small trees, completely covering them, weakening and killing them by preventing photosynthesis.

- **Wintercreeper** (*Euonymus fortunei*) and **English ivy** (*Hedera helix*) grow along the ground in extensive ropey networks, forming dense monocultures that push out and exclude native plants. These vines also climb trees by attaching to the bark, adding weight that greatly increases the likelihood of toppling. English ivy completely engulfs trees, covering all branches and blocking sunlight, weakening and killing trees within several years. The effects are magnified because as evergreen vines, their foliage remains all year long.

- **Chinese and Japanese wisteria** (*Wisteria sinensis* and *W. floribunda*) and **Asian bittersweet** (*Celastrus orbiculatus*) are strong woody vines that coil tightly around trees as they climb, killing by girdling, which cuts off the flow of water and nutrients. The significant weight of these vines can also lead to toppling.

Japanese Wisteria

Jil Swearingen

TERRESTRIAL PLANTS

GRASSES & SEDGES

JOINT-HEAD GRASS

Arthraxon hispidus (Thunb.) Makino / Grass family (Poaceae)

© Judy Fulton

Jil Swearingen

Origin—Temperate and tropical Africa, Asia, Australia

Background—Joint-head grass, also known as small carpetgrass and hairy joint-grass, may have been introduced to the U.S. from Japan for the 1876 International Exhibition in Philadelphia and subsequently spread through packing material and garden escapes. By 1935, the grass was widely distributed from Pennsylvania to Florida.

Distribution & Habitat—Joint-head grass has been reported as invasive in natural areas from Massachusetts to Florida and Kansas to Texas. It favors sunny, moist conditions and is found on floodplains, shorelines, and streambanks, as well as along roads and trails. It does not tolerate low pH soils.

Ecological Threat—Joint-head grass displaces native plants and reduces biodiversity. It poses a particular threat to the federally endangered harperella (*Ptilimnium nodosum*) because the invasive grass forms dense clumps and competes with harperella for limited habitat at the water's edge and in shallow stream environments.

DESCRIPTION & BIOLOGY

Plant. Annual sprawling grass with upright branching stems 2–3' high that root at lower nodes. Mature clumps have a feathery appearance.

Leaves. Blades are bright green, up to 3" long by ¾" wide, egg-shaped, blunt-tipped, undulate, with cordate (heart-shaped) bases that clasp around the stem. Blade margins and sheath are visibly hairy with short white bristles, and the sheath is covered with wart-like nodules.

Flowers, fruits & seeds. Flowers are in terminal finger-like clusters ½–1¾" long, are green to red or purple; occur late summer to fall. Fruits are yellowish achenes (dry one-seeded, non-dehiscing fruits); mature in fall.

Method of spread. Distant spread is by achenes dispersed by moving water and by new shoots formed from nodes touching the ground.

Look-alikes. Non-native and invasive wavyleaf basketgrass (*Oplismenus undulatifolius*) with longer, distinctly rippled leaves and sticky achenes and Japanese stiltgrass (*Microstegium vimineum*) with slender asymmetrical leaves with a silvery midrib; native deertongue panicgrass (*Dichanthelium clandestinum*) with shorter ovate leaf blades and sheaths with rough bumps, like a deer's tongue.

Prevention & Control—Do not plant or spread joint-head grass through soil on shoes, tires, or other items. Clean boots when leaving infested areas. Plants are easily pulled by hand, and should be bagged and removed when achenes are present. For large infestations, a contact or systemic herbicide may be needed.

Jil Swearingen

Native Alternatives—Deertongue panicgrass (*Dichanthelium clandestinum*) or a mix of native grasses and forbs.

CHINESE FOUNTAIN GRASS

Cenchrus purpurascens Thunb. / Grass family (Poaceae)

Origin—Eastern temperate and tropical Asia, Australia

Background—Chinese fountain grass (synonym *Pennisetum alopecuroides*) was introduced as an ornamental in the 1880s–1900s. It escapes from cultivation and is spreading into natural areas. Cultivars are sold in a wide range of growth heights (1–5'), flower colors (purples, pinks, or whites), and autumn foliage colors.

© Judy Fulton

© Judy Fulton

Distribution & Habitat—Chinese fountain grass is currently reported as invasive in scattered locations in the mid-Atlantic region (Maryland, New Jersey, and Virginia) and in isolated locations in Illinois, Kentucky, North Carolina, and Massachusetts. It prefers moist, well-drained soils in full sun, but is somewhat shade and drought tolerant.

Ecological Threat—Chinese fountain grass forms dense patches, pushes out native plants and takes over disturbed areas and openings, preventing other plants from establishing. Birds are attracted to the seeds, but the nutritional value is not understood.

DESCRIPTION & BIOLOGY

Plant. A warm-season, clump-forming perennial grass that grows 2–5' tall.

Leaves. Leaf blades are up to ½" wide, erect or drooping and either flat, folded lengthwise or spiral-twisting; green in summer, changing to golden yellow in fall, and fading to beige late fall through winter.

Flowers, fruits & seeds. Flowers in dense, bristly, "bottle brush" spikes that are silvery, pinkish-white to purple and arch outwardly from the clump in late summer, like water spraying from a fountain. Flower spikes turn brownish as the achenes (dry one-seeded fruits) mature, usually persisting until late fall or early winter before shattering to disperse seeds nearby.

Method of spread. Distant spread is by achenes and seeds moved by rushing water or carried on muddy shoes, tires, equipment, animal feet, and other surfaces. Local spread is through natural "shattering" release of achenes that disperses seeds nearby.

Look-alikes. Crimson fountain grass (*Cenchrus setaceus*)—a long-established invasive weed in western, southwestern, and southern states, and more recently reported as invasive in the mid-Atlantic (District of Columbia, Maryland, and Virginia)—with long, narrow, beige-purple, dense "bottle brush" inflorescences.

Prevention & Control—Do not purchase or plant Chinese fountain grass or crimson fountain grass. Cut off flower stalks and bag them for disposal in a landfill to prevent the spread of seeds. Dig up plants and put in a dedicated invasive plant waste pile or bag and dispose of them in a landfill.

Native Alternatives—Bottlebrush grass (*Elymus hystrix*) and other grasses.

JAPANESE STILTGRASS
Microstegium vimineum (Trin.) A. Camus / Grass family (Poaceae)

Jil Swearingen © Judy Fulton

Origin—Japan, Korea, China, Malaysia, India

Background—Japanese stiltgrass was used as a packing material for porcelain imported to the U.S. It was discovered in the wild around 1919, likely as the result of seed being accidentally dropped outdoors.

Distribution & Habitat—Japanese stiltgrass has been reported as invasive in natural areas from Wisconsin to Texas and New Hampshire to Florida. It grows in partially shaded road banks, fire trails and logging roads, mesic and floodplain forests, streambanks, river bluffs, utility rights-of-way, ditches, thickets, and early successional fields. Stiltgrass can be found in full sun to deep shade and in moist, rich soils high in nitrogen. It readily invades floodplains prone to natural scouring and areas subject to mowing, tilling, and white-tailed deer traffic.

© Judy Fulton

Ecological Threat—Stiltgrass displaces native herbaceous and woody plants, makes soils more basic, and increases soil nitrate availability. It often co-occurs with the highly invasive shrub Japanese barberry (*Berberis thunbergii*). According to a 2020 report (Miller et al.), stiltgrass was found to be the most aggressive invader of national park forests in the eastern U.S. and is a high management priority.

DESCRIPTION & BIOLOGY

Plant. Annual, shallow-rooted, sprawling grass, 1–4' tall, with thin, wiry stems, supported by stilt-like prop roots and interconnected by a horizontal runner stem from which the roots emerge. Dead stems remain through the winter and form a dense, matted layer of thatch on the ground. Stiltgrass germinates in the spring and grows steadily, reaching maturity in late summer.

Leaves. Pale green, lance-shaped, asymmetrical, about 3" long by ¾" wide, with a **silvery midrib** and hairy sheath margins.

Flowers, fruits & seeds. Two flower forms: *chasmogamous* (exposed) wind-pollinated terminal flowers; *cleistogamous* (hidden) self-fertilizing flowers within leaf axils. Three-branched flower spikes, 1–2" long, emerge in late summer. The fruit is an awned, bristly achene (dry one-seeded fruit). A single plant can produce up to 1,000 seeds that remain viable in the soil for up to five years and germinate readily following soil disturbance.

Method of spread. Distant spread is by seed carried by animals, rain and surface water, and in gravel, mulch, soil, nursery-grown plants, and mud on shoes and tires. Local spread is through seed and vegetative growth of new plants from stem nodes.

Look-alikes. Native white grass (*Leersia virginica*), Virginia cutgrass (*Leersia oryzoides*), nimblewill (*Muhlenbergia schreberi*), and other grasses.

Prevention & Control—Do not spread Japanese stiltgrass to uninfested sites. Because Japanese stiltgrass can be confused with some native grasses, it is important to know how to recognize and identify it. Attention to new infestations should be a priority. Stiltgrass can be pulled by hand at any time of the year. If achenes or seeds are present, plants should be bagged and removed. Cutting is not generally recommended because plants cut early in the growing season will regrow and produce flowers and seeds. For extensive infestations, a contact herbicide may be needed.

Native Alternatives—Native grasses or a mix of native grasses and forbs.

CHINESE SILVER GRASS

Miscanthus sinensis Andersson / Grass family (Poaceae)

© Bill Johnson

© Judy Fulton

Origin—Southeast Asia

Background—Chinese silver grass, also known as Japanese silver grass, maiden grass, and miscanthus, was introduced to the U.S. in the late 1800s as an ornamental. It is frequently planted in commercial, residential and public landscapes. More than 50 forms of Chinese silver grass are sold in the U.S. nursery trade. Isolated plants set little or no seed due to self-incompatibility; wind-blown pollen from other forms is needed in order to produce viable seed.

Distribution & Habitat—Chinese silver grass has been increasingly reported in natural areas as invasive in the eastern U.S. as well as Missouri, Louisiana, California and Colorado. It invades roadsides, forest edges, old fields, and other disturbed areas. It prefers full sun and is adapted to well-drained, nutrient-poor soils on roadsides, powerline rights-of-way, and steep embankments.

© Judy Fulton

Ecological Threat—Chinese silver grass is an opportunistic invader and can quickly spread over open disturbed areas, pushing out native plants. Its large size and dense growth allow it to dominate areas. It is extremely flammable and is recognized as a wildland fire hazard.

DESCRIPTION & BIOLOGY

Plant. A warm-season, clumping, rhizomatous perennial grass up to 8' tall with inflorescences extending above the leaves. Due to the large number of Chinese silver grass forms planted, the wild type now produces a significant amount of viable seed.

Leaves. Basal, slender, 7–30" long, upright or somewhat arching, with silvery midribs, sharp tips, and rough margins. Some cultivars have variegated blades with whitish, vertical or uneven crosswise stripes.

Flowers, fruits & seeds. Flowers are silvery to pink, in fingerlike terminal panicles about 1' long on flower stalks up to 8' tall. Flowering occurs September to November. Fruits (achenes) are about 1/8" long and rough with a twisted bristle tip. Initially pale pink to reddish in color, achenes gradually turn tan in fall and persist through winter.

Method of spread. Distant spread is by wind-dispersed seed and rhizomes. Local spread is by seed and rhizomes.

Look-alikes. Invasive ravenna grass (*Tripidium ravennae*), pampas grass (*Cortaderia selloana*), and giant cane (*Arundo donax*), and possibly some tall native grasses like big bluestem (*Andropogon gerardi*) and eastern gama grass (*Tripsacum dactyloides*).

Prevention & Control—Do not purchase or plant Chinese silver grass. Cut off flower stalks and bag them for disposal in a landfill to prevent the spread of seeds. Dig up plants and put in a dedicated invasive plant waste pile, or bag and dispose of them in a landfill.

Native Alternatives—Native grasses like eastern gama grass (*Tripsacum dactyloides*), Indian grass (*Sorghastrum nutans*), broomsedge (*Andropogon virginicus*), and little bluestem (*Schizachyrium scoparium*).

WAVYLEAF BASKETGRASS
Oplismenus undulatifolius (Ard.) P. Beauv. / Grass family (Poaceae)

Jil Swearingen

Jil Swearingen

Origin—Southern Europe, Southeast Asia

Background—A few small patches of wavyleaf basketgrass (synonym *Oplismenus hirtellus* ssp. *undulatifolius*) were discovered by Edward Uebel in 1997 in Patapsco Valley State Park, Ellicott City, Maryland. The original source of the plants is unknown.

Distribution & Habitat—Wavyleaf basketgrass has been reported as invasive in natural areas in Maryland, Pennsylvania, West Virginia and the District of Columbia. A single patch was eradicated from Delaware in 2018. It prefers forest interiors and edges, and is highly shade-adapted.

Ecological Threat—Wavyleaf basketgrass forms dense patches across the forest floor, displacing native plants. It often co-occurs with invasive Japanese stiltgrass and can grow in deeper leaf litter than stiltgrass.

DESCRIPTION & BIOLOGY

Plant. Shallow-rooted perennial grass that produces long stolons, and branches and roots at lower stem nodes.

Leaves. About 1½–4" long by ½" wide with undulating ripples across the leaf surface. The leaf sheath and stem have conspicuous short hairs.

Flowers, fruits & seeds. Flowers are in spikelets that alternate along the flowering stalk; lower bracts have very long awns. Flowering begins in July. Fruits (achenes) appear in late summer and exude a natural glue-like substance which makes them *extremely sticky*.

Method of spread. Distant spread is by sticky achenes that adhere to animal fur, clothing, shoes, tires, and many other items. Seeds and achenes can also be moved in soil and gravel. Local spread is by seed, stolons, and new plants that form at stem nodes.

Look-alikes. Native deertongue panicgrass (*Dichanthelium clandestinum*) and non-native invasive joint-head grass (*Arthraxon hispidus*).

Prevention & Control—Do not plant wavyleaf or any basketgrass in the mid-Atlantic states. Stay out of infested areas from August through November to limit seed dispersal. If you work in an infested area, remove all seeds from shoes, clothing, and equipment prior to leaving.

Native Alternatives—Deertongue grass (*Dichanthelium clandestinum*), bottlebrush grass (*Elymus hystrix*), little bluestem (*Schizachyrium scoparium*), and many other native grasses.

EUROPEAN COMMON REED

Phragmites australis (Cav.) Trin. ex Steud. ssp. *australis* / Grass family (Poaceae)

Origin—Europe

Background—European forms of *Phragmites* were probably introduced to North America by accident in ballast material in the late 1700s or early 1800s. Recent research using genetic markers has demonstrated that three separate lineages occur in North America: one endemic (i.e., native) and widespread, one with uncertain nativity that occurs across the southern U.S. from California to Florida and into Mexico and Central America ('Gulf Coast' type), and an introduced invasive from Europe, which is the focus of this section. The European *Phragmites* first became established along the Atlantic coast and then spread across the continent over the course of the 20th century. The native form was historically

© Judy Fulton   Jil Swearingen

more widespread, occurring throughout Canada and most of the U.S., except for the Southeast; it remains fairly widespread throughout the western U.S.

Distribution & Habitat—European common reed has been reported as invasive in natural areas throughout the conterminous U.S. It inhabits disturbed to pristine wet areas including tidal and non-tidal wetlands; brackish and freshwater marshes; river, lake and pond edges; and roadsides and ditches. European common reed prefers full sun and can tolerate fresh to mesohaline salinities.

Ecological Threat—European common reed is a vigorously growing plant that forms dense monotypic stands, occupying all available growing space and pushing out other plants, including the native subspecies. The invasive also alters wetland hydrology, increases the potential for fire, and reduces and degrades wetland wildlife habitat due in part to its very dense growth habit. There is currently no evidence of hybridization between native and introduced forms.

DESCRIPTION & BIOLOGY

Plant. Perennial grass, 16–20' tall, somewhat rough to the touch, stems may have **mildew** but *lack fungal spots*.

Leaves. Blue-green, typically up to 1½" wide; *ligule less than 1 mm long;* leaf sheaths adhere tightly to the stem and persist through winter.

Flowers, fruits & seeds. Flowers are in tan to purplish bushy panicles; spikelets are about ½–¾" long, with upper glumes ⅕–⅖" long, lower glumes ¹⁄₁₀–³⁄₁₀" (most less than ²⁄₁₀"), and lemmas ³⁄₁₀–⁶⁄₁₀" long.

GRASSES & SEDGES

Method of spread. Distant spread is by seed dispersed by wind and water, and by offsite movement of rhizome fragments. Local spread is through growth of rhizomes and stolons.

Look-alikes. Native *Phragmites australis* ssp. *americanus* and other tall grasses.

Prevention & Control—Avoid spread of European common reed to uninfested areas. Phragmites is very difficult to dig up, but can be managed with systemic herbicide formulated for aquatic environments. Two stem-mining moths (*Archanara*) have been petitioned for release in the U.S. as biocontrols.

Native Alternatives—Big cordgrass (*Spartina cynosuroides*) and wild rice (*Zizania aquatica*).

BAMBOO

Golden bamboo (*Phyllostachys aurea* Rivière & C. Rivière), Yellow-groove bamboo (*Phyllostachys aureosulcata* McClure), Bisset bamboo (*Phyllostachys bissetii* McClure), Arrow bamboo (*Pseudosasa japonica* (Siebold & Zucc. ex Steud.) Makino ex Nakai)

Arrow bamboo

Arrow bamboo

Origin—Asia

Background—These four running bamboos (i.e., bamboos that spread underground by tough, thick rhizomes) are woody, reed-like grasses and popular ornamentals. They have been reported as invasive in natural areas. Other potentially invasive species and cultivars are also available in the nursery trade. An increasing number of mid-Atlantic and northeastern jurisdictions have laws, regulations and ordinances that prohibit or restrict the use or sale of running bamboo. Most of these also require owners to keep existing bamboo from neighboring properties and to remove it if it has crossed onto another property.

© Judy Fulton

Yellow-groove bamboo

The uncontrolled spread of these bamboos is increasingly leading to lawsuits filed by homeowners against their neighbors due to bamboo's ability to destroy human structures and landscaping.

Distribution & Habitat—These four bamboo species have been reported as invasive in natural areas in mid-Atlantic and southern states, as well as in Connecticut, New York, and California. Infestations are often associated with residences from which they have escaped. Yellow-groove is most common in this range and is often misidentified as golden bamboo.

Ecological Threat—Bamboos can form very dense clonal stands that displace native plant species and suppress the growth and regeneration of native plant communities. Cut or split culms can allow water to collect, creating breeding habitat for mosquitoes. Bamboo stands are often used by birds whose droppings grow a fungus that causes histoplasmosis, a disease affecting mammals.

DESCRIPTION & BIOLOGY

Plant. Woody evergreen perennial grasses with stiff stems (also called culms or canes) that have solid ring-like joints (nodes) and hollow internodes. Leaves and branches emerge from nodes and alternate along the culm. A bamboo thicket or stand is a single plant composed of many culms. Bamboos produce new shoots each spring that grow in height and diameter for about 60 days, becoming culms that produce leaves. After that 2-month growth period, an individual bamboo culm never grows in height or diameter again and may live for about a decade. Unlike woody broadleaf plants, bamboos do not produce secondary growth, and typically shed and grow new foliage each year. Bamboos are colonial plants, relying on energy from current canes to produce new shoots and increase root growth. Most bamboo species need about three years to become established, after which more and bigger culms are produced each spring as the colony grows into a large, mature stand. The time to maturity and maximum size varies from 4 to 15 years according to the species and the soil, sunlight, moisture and climate conditions.

Arrow bamboo has narrow culms ¼–½" wide, with one branch per node and nodes surrounded by bristly hairs; canes grow to 10–20' tall. Golden, yellow-groove, and Bisset bamboo have thick culms ranging from 1–2" in diameter, with two unequal branches and a groove (sulcus) alternating at each node; canes grow to 20–30' or taller. The sulcus of yellow-groove bamboo is yellow, at least on newer canes, but the color often fades over time.

Leaves. Arrow bamboo leaves are tough and papery with a short petiole; lanceolate with a tapered, fine-pointed tip; finely grooved on upper and lower surfaces, with pubescent hairs on the grooves of lower surfaces; and leaf margins with tiny teeth that feel rough to the touch. The leaves range in size from 5–13" long by 1–1¾" wide, depending on the age of the colony, and occur singly and spread out along the culm, and more tightly together at the culm tip. Golden, yellow-groove and Bisset bamboo leaves are tough and papery to leathery, 3–7" long by 1¾" wide, lance-shaped with a pointed tip and a hairy leaf base.

Flowers, fruits & seeds. Flowering is infrequent and unpredictable, sometimes in 15- to 60-year-old plants; flowers are grasslike and not especially showy.

Method of spread. Local spread is by vegetative means through vigorous rhizomatous growth. A single *Phyllostachys* plant can grow outward as much as 20' a year in all directions to cover a large area. Because arrow bamboo and the three *Phyllostachys* species can grow from a single node on a stem or rhizome fragment, they can spread from improperly managed stands, discarded waste, and pieces of bamboo plants washed away by storms.

Look-alikes. There are no *Phyllostachys* or other large bamboos native to the U.S. However, the smaller arrow bamboo (*Pseudosasa japonica*) can be confused with three native bamboo species: giant cane (*Arundinaria gigantea*) that occurs in the Mid-Atlantic (Virginia and West Virginia), the Southeast, and the Midwest; switch cane (*Arundinaria tecta*) that occurs in the Mid-Atlantic (Maryland and Virginia) and the Southeast; and hill cane (*Arundinaria appalachiana*) that occurs in the Southeast.

Prevention & Control—Do not purchase or plant exotic bamboo. Ensure the destruction or proper disposal of all parts of removed bamboo. Once established, running bamboo can be very difficult to eradicate due to its extensive underground rhizomatous network and ability to regrow from a single overlooked node. Bamboo can be eradicated through excavation of soil with heavy equipment as long as every single rhizome piece is removed. While control of relatively young bamboo by manually digging out rhizomes is possible, eliminating mature stands with this method is extremely labor-intensive and will need to be continued for years to ensure complete eradication. Mowing or cutting is generally ineffective because the underground network will accelerate its growth outward and new culms will emerge from the tough rhizomes. Control with systemic herbicides, with or without digging, is more practical and can be very effective. To a certain extent, bamboo can be contained by encircling plantings with deep trenching or barriers specifically manufactured and slanted for bamboo, followed by diligent monitoring to ensure no rhizomes grow over or escape. Before attempting to control bamboo, carefully research the proper method for eradicating the type you have. When considering hiring a service to control the bamboo, look for an experienced company that specializes in bamboo removal. Improper control can lead to resurgence of the bamboo and make the infestation worse.

Golden bamboo

Native Alternatives—Many woody and herbaceous species.

BOG BULRUSH

Schoenoplectiella mucronata (L.) J. Jung & H.K. Choi / Sedge family (Cyperaceae)

Origin—Africa, Asia, Australia, Europe

Background—Bog bulrush (synonyms *Schoenoplectus mucronatus* and *Scirpus mucronatus*), is also known as rough-seed bulrush and rice marsh bulrush. It was first observed in the U.S. in New England in the early 1900s, but did not persist. One report in the Midwest suggests that bog bulrush may have been introduced to a local pond by way of contaminated ornamental lilies planted at the site. Bog bulrush is considered one of the world's worst weeds because it is a major pest in rice fields.

Distribution & Habitat—Bog bulrush has been reported as invasive in natural areas in Delaware and the eastern shore of Maryland, and in scattered locations in California, Illinois, Indiana, Missouri, New York, Oregon and Washington. It occurs in wet soil in freshwater ponds and ditches.

Wayne Longbottom

© Judy Fulton

Ecological Threat—Bog bulrush invades wetland habitats, generally ones that have been disturbed.

DESCRIPTION & BIOLOGY

Plant. Annual or perennial wetland sedge to 3' high, with sharp triangular stems (culms) that may bend or droop near the tip; annual form has fibrous roots; perennial form has short, hard rhizomes. It reproduces by seed, rhizomes, stolons, and tubers. Round, dark tubers form at the tips of stolons and, when constantly submerged, can grow into new plants; when conditions are unfavorable, the tubers go dormant, but can sprout when conditions improve.

Leaves. Triangular bladeless sheaths wrapped around the base of the culm; 1–2 leaves per culm.

Flowers, fruits & seeds. Flowers occur in June in radiating clusters of pine cone-like spikelets emerging near the stem tip. Each spikelet contains several dozen individual flowers; each flower is covered by a green scale with brown margins and a small pointed tip. Fruiting occurs summer to fall. The fruit is an achene about 1/16" long by 1/32" wide, dark brown to blackish when mature.

Method of spread. By seeds, tubers, rhizomes and stolons.

Look-alikes. Native blunt-scale or weak-stalk bulrush (*Schoenoplectus purshianus*), Olney three-square (*Schoenoplectus americanus*), common threesquare bulrush (*Schoenoplectus pungens*), and other sedges.

Prevention & Control—Do not purchase or plant bog bulrush. Manual removal has been shown to be effective, especially when the entire plant, including rhizomes, stolons, and tubers are included. If flowers or fruits are present, clip and bag the seed heads and dispose of them in a landfill—not in a mulch pile, where they can survive. For large infestations with significant root masses, it may be necessary to use a systemic herbicide that kills the entire plant including the roots and avoids soil disturbance. When moving between sites, equipment should be inspected and cleaned by power washing to remove seeds and tubers.

Native Alternatives—Common rush (*Juncus effusus*), woolgrass (*Scirpus cyperinus*), and various true sedges like tussock sedge (*Carex stricta*) and sallow sedge (*Carex lurida*) that like wet feet.

RAVENNA GRASS
Tripidium ravennae (L.) H. Scholz / Grass family (Poaceae)

© Bill Johnson

Origin—Southern Europe, North Africa, western Asia

Background—Ravenna grass (synonyms *Saccharum ravennae*, *Erianthus ravennae*, and *Ripidium ravennae*) is also known as plume grass. It was introduced to the U.S. as an ornamental and reported in the horticultural trade as early as 1921. It is escaping and invading natural areas from plantings.

Distribution & Habitat—Ravenna grass has been reported as invasive in natural areas in scattered locations in the mid-Atlantic and southern U.S., and more extensively in the Southwest and West. It is designated a noxious weed in a number of states. Ravenna grass invades roadsides, fields, riparian areas and various disturbed locations. It is drought-tolerant, somewhat shade-tolerant and grows well in moist soils.

Ecological Threat—Ravenna grass has been described as being highly competitive and providing little bird and wildlife cover. It competes with and displaces native plants and is an invasive threat to sunny riparian areas.

DESCRIPTION & BIOLOGY

Plant. A tall, perennial, rhizomatous, clumping grass with a basal tuft of leaves and flowering stalks that reach heights of 8–12' or more. Individual grasses can form clumps or tussocks several feet across. Stems (i.e., culms) turn reddish as the plants mature.

Leaves. Two forms: *Basal* leaves are gray-green, 3–4' long by ½–1" wide, and have a bright white mid-vein; the upper side of the leaf base is densely covered with long, fuzzy, tannish-yellow, irritating hairs. *Stem* leaves are shorter than the basal leaves and continue up the length of the culm to the base of the inflorescence.

Flowers, fruits & seeds. Flowers occur in late summer and fall in pale, silvery, feathery plumes at the tips of tall stalks; plumes turn a purplish color when mature. Inflorescences are lance-shaped panicles about 1–2½' long; each panicle is composed of small branchlets with silvery flower spikelets. Spikelets occur in unequal pairs with the lower spikelet sessile and the upper spikelet stalked. A single panicle can produce thousands of achenes.

Method of spread. Distant spread is by seeds dispersed by wind and water. Local spread is also by seed.

Look-alikes. Native big cordgrass (*Spartina cynosuroides*), native and invasive subspecies of common reed (*Phragmites australis*), invasive giant cane (*Arundo donax*), Chinese silver grass (*Miscanthus sinensis*), and other tall grasses.

Prevention & Control—Ravenna grass is clumping and not strongly rhizomatous. It can be pulled out by hand or removed mechanically. All roots need to be removed to prevent resprouting. Removal should be done before the plants go to seed to prevent dispersal of seeds. Wear long sleeves, long pants, gloves, and a mask to avoid the irritating hairs.

Native Alternatives—Eastern gama grass (*Tripsacum dactyloides*), Indian grass (*Sorghastrum nutans*), sugarcane plumegrass (*Saccharum giganteum*) and other native grasses.

FORBS

GARLIC MUSTARD
Alliaria petiolata (M. Bieb.) Cavara & Grande / Mustard family (Brassicaceae)

Leslie Mehrhoff, bugwood.org

© Judy Fulton

Origin—Europe

Background—Garlic mustard was first recorded in the U.S. on Long Island, New York, around 1868. It was probably introduced by settlers for food and medicinal purposes.

Distribution & Habitat—Garlic mustard has been reported as invasive in natural areas from Minnesota to Arkansas and Maine to South Carolina, as well as in scattered locations in the western U.S. Intolerant of highly acidic soils, it is found in moist to dry habitats in young forests, forest openings, forest edges, floodplains, roadsides and various disturbed lands.

Ecological Threat—Garlic mustard forms monocultures that shade out and displace native spring ephemeral wildflower communities of species like spring beauty (*Claytonia virginica*), yellow trout-lily (*Erythronium americanum*), and cutleaf toothwort (*Cardamine concatenata*). Garlic mustard also releases allelopathic chemicals that inhibit the growth of other plants and can kill mycorrhizal fungi associated with native trees, suppressing tree seedling growth. Garlic mustard replaces toothworts (*Cardamine*) which are important host plants for native **West Virginia White** (*Pieris virginiensis*), **Mustard White** (*Pieris oleracea*), and **Falcate Orange-tip** (*Anthocharis midea*) butterflies. Chemicals in garlic mustard are toxic to the larvae of these butterflies and are leading to reductions in the populations of these insects. White-tailed deer facilitate the expansion of garlic mustard by preferentially feeding on native plants.

© Judy Fulton

© Judy Fulton

DESCRIPTION & BIOLOGY

Plant. Biennial herb with a branched taproot: first-year plants are low, overwintering rosettes of leaves; second-year plants produce single or multiple flowering stalks 1–4' high that die back by late spring. Dried fruiting stalks persist for many months. Crushed fresh stems and leaves smell like garlic (*Allium sativum*). The leaves contain trace amounts of cyanide—presumably to deter herbivores. Boiling leaves in water removes much of the toxin and makes them edible for humans.

Leaves. Two forms: first-year leaves are basal and heart-shaped with scalloped margins; second-year leaves alternate along the flowering stems and are more triangular-shaped with pointed tips and toothed margins.

Flowers, fruits & seeds. Flowers are white, with four petals, and occur in small, dense clusters at the tips of stems. Fruits are slender erect capsules called siliques. Seeds are about 1/10" long, slender, tan when young and black when mature. A single garlic mustard plant can produce hundreds of seeds that can survive in the soil for up to ten years.

Method of spread. Distant spread is by seed carried by water and people.

Look-alikes. White-flowered native species including toothworts (*Cardamine*), sweet cicely (*Osmorhiza claytonii*), wild anise (*Osmorhiza longistylis*), and early saxifrage (*Micrantha virginiensis*). First-year leaves of garlic mustard look similar to those of native golden ragwort (*Packera aurea*) and non-native invasive ground ivy (*Glechoma hederacea*), henbit and purple dead nettle (*Lamium amplexicaule, L. purpureum*).

Prevention & Control—Effective management requires a long-term effort. Hand-removal of entire plants including the roots is effective for light, scattered infestations. Flowering and non-flowering plants can be pulled and placed in high traffic areas (e.g., trails) or piled in designated spots that can be monitored in following years. If fruits are present, the stalks should be clipped, bagged and disposed of in a landfill. Cutting flowering plants is not recommended because the plants will sprout from the roots and continue to produce flowers. Treatment with herbicides may be effective, but will need to be repeated for multiple years. A root-crown mining weevil (*Ceutorhynchus scrobicollis*) has been proposed for release as a biological control agent in the U.S.

Native Alternatives—Native spring ephemeral wildflower species.

ITALIAN ARUM

Arum italicum Mill. / Arum family (Araceae)

© Judy Fulton

Origin—Africa, Asia, Europe

Background—Italian arum, also known as Italian lords and ladies, orange candle plant, and cuckoo pint, was introduced as an ornamental for its attractive foliage, flowers and fruits. It is grown indoors as a houseplant and in gardens, where it is sometimes installed under other plants to maintain winter greenery when deciduous plants die back. There are several subspecies and cultivars in the trade.

Distribution & Habitat—Italian arum has been reported as invasive in the District of Columbia, Maryland, and Virginia, and in other states including Alabama, California, Illinois, Indiana, Missouri, North Carolina, Oregon, Tennessee, and Washington. It thrives in moist humus-rich soil in shaded forest or edge habitats but can tolerate drought.

Ecological Threat—Italian arum escapes from gardens into natural areas, where it displaces native plants. Its abundant underground tubers and wildlife-dispersed fruits make it extremely difficult to eradicate once established. All parts of the plant are poisonous due to calcium oxalate crystals that can cause skin irritation and swelling of the tongue and throat.

DESCRIPTION & BIOLOGY

Plant. Herbaceous perennial growing 1–1½' high from underground tubers.

Leaves. Basal, arrow-shaped, up to 1' long, glossy green with white veins and long petioles. Leaves emerge in the fall, and remain through the winter into spring, dying back in summer. In colder climates, the leaves die back in the winter and new ones emerge in the spring before dying back in summer. Newly emerging plants have small heart-shaped leaves.

Flowers, fruits & seeds. Male and female flowers are tiny and occur on a pale yellow to cream-colored stalk (spadix) surrounded by a pale green-colored leaf-like sheath (spathe). Flowering occurs in the spring. Male flowers produce heat that aids in pollination. Fruits are berries that form on the spadix in summer and turn from green to red when mature.

Method of spread. Distant spread is by birds and other wildlife that eat the fruits and deposit berries or seeds in new places; by people who plant and move contaminated soil, mulch, gravel and other materials containing fruits, seeds or tubers; and by flood events. Local spread is by tubers and by seeds dispersed by ants.

Look-alikes. Other members of the Arum family including native Jack-in-the-pulpit (*Arisaema triphyllum*), green dragon (*Arisaema dracontium*), skunk cabbage (*Symplocarpus foetidus*), and arrow arum (*Peltandra virginica*); and non-native ornamentals like calla lily (*Zantedeschia aethiopica*).

Prevention & Control—Do not purchase, plant or share Italian arum with others. Early detection and removal will help prevent it from establishing in new locations. Wear gloves when working with this plant. Control of this species is extremely difficult once it gets a foothold. Cut and bag flower stalks before the berries ripen to prevent spread by seed. Dig up plants, removing all the tubers, including those deep in the soil. Monitor regularly for new sprouts and continue to remove tubers as new plants appear. Do not move soil from infested sites. All plant parts and nearby soil should be bagged and disposed of in the trash, not mixed with yard waste or home compost. Italian arum is resistant to many herbicides and requires specialized mixture to achieve effective control.

Native Alternatives—Jack-in-the-pulpit (*Arisaema triphyllum*) and green dragon (*Arisaema dracontium*).

SPOTTED KNAPWEED

Centaurea stoebe L. ssp. *australis* (Pančić ex A. Kern.) Greuter / Aster family (Asteraceae)

© Judy Fulton

© Judy Fulton

Origin—Europe, western Asia

Background—Spotted knapweed was accidentally introduced into North America in the late 1800s in contaminated alfalfa and clover seed and in soil used for ship ballast.

Distribution & Habitat—Spotted knapweed has been reported as invasive in every state in the continental U.S. with most populations in the West, Great Lakes, Northeast and Mid-Atlantic regions. It grows in a wide variety of habitats, including open forests, shale and serpentine barrens, meadows, prairies, old fields, and various disturbed areas. Spotted knapweed prefers full sun and can tolerate nutrient-poor soils and harsh, dry conditions.

Ecological Threat—Spotted knapweed forms deep taproots that enable it to capture moisture and nutrients and spread rapidly, displacing native vegetation and reducing forage for wildlife and livestock.

DESCRIPTION & BIOLOGY

Plant. Herbaceous biennial or perennial. In North America, plants can live three to nine years or longer and regrow from buds on their root crowns. Individual plants are capable of producing an estimated 500–4,000 seeds per square foot each year; most of the seed is viable at the time of dispersal and can remain in the soil for up to 8 years.

Leaves. A basal rosette of deeply-lobed, stalked leaves, each about 8" long, is produced the first year; stem leaves are alternate and may be slightly lobed or linear; leaves become smaller and less lobed toward the top of the stem.

Flowers, fruits & seeds. Flowers are produced in early summer, in the second or later year, and consist of small oval-shaped bases covered by green leafy bracts with dark pointed tips adorned with black eyelash-like trichomes; the bases are topped by heads of pink to light purple disc flowers and showy, dissected ray flower petals. The dark tips of the bracts give the spotted look for which the plant is named. Flowering stems are up to 4' tall and branched. The fruit is an achene (a dry one-seeded, non-dehiscent fruit), about ⅛" long, blackish-green with pale vertical lines, 1–2 whorls of minutely barbed, flattened bristles at the broad end, and a tiny elaiosome at the narrow end.

Method of spread. Most seed is dropped near the parent plant and may be dispersed locally by ants. Seed can be spread great distances by equipment and machinery used in farming, logging, road construction and other activities; by wind and water; by wildlife, livestock and vehicles traveling through infested areas; and by contaminated crop seed, hay, gravel, and soil.

Look-alikes. Native and non-native thistles, including invasive Canada thistle (*Cirsium arvense*).

Prevention & Control—The most effective management strategy for spotted knapweed is to prevent spread to uninfested areas by: 1) avoiding travel through infested areas; 2) cleaning footwear, clothing, backpacks, and other items after hiking through infested areas; and 3) using certified weed-free hay. Individual plants can be dug up using a shovel or weed-popper type tool when the soil is moist, ensuring that the entire crown and taproot are removed. Control of spotted knapweed infestations is difficult and usually requires a long-term commitment of time, labor and materials.

Native Alternatives—Native thistles which are important host plants and nectar plants for native insects.

CANADA THISTLE

Cirsium arvense (L.) Scop. / Aster family (Asteraceae)

© Judy Fulton

© Judy Fulton

Origin—Europe, Asia

Background—Canada thistle, also called creeping thistle, was accidentally introduced to North America in the 1600s and is designated as a noxious weed in 43 states.

Distribution & Habitat—Canada thistle is an extremely widespread weed of agricultural and ecological areas in the U.S., occurring throughout the northern states and Southwest. It is largely absent in the southern states from Texas to Georgia. It invades a variety of dry to moist open habitats including barrens, fields, glades, grasslands, pastures, streambanks, wet meadows, wet prairies, and open forests. It is not very tolerant of shade.

Ecological Threat—Canada thistle can form dense stands that shade out and displace native plants, change plant community structure and species composition, and reduce biodiversity. It spreads rapidly and is very difficult to control once established.

DESCRIPTION & BIOLOGY

Plant. Erect perennial forb to 4' tall, with smooth or slightly hairy stems and extensive root system.

Leaves. Alternate, lance-shaped, 2–6" long, irregularly lobed with few to many prickles on margins.

Flowers, fruits & seeds. Urn-shaped, flat-bottomed inflorescences covered by dozens of purple, pointed bracts and topped by a pom-pom of individual pink disc flowers. Flowering occurs late June through August. Fruits and seeds (i.e., achenes) are 1/16-1/8" long with a feathery pappus.

Method of spread. Distant spread is by wind-dispersed achenes, and local expansion is through growth of rhizomes and rhizome fragments.

Look-alikes. Numerous native and exotic thistle and knapweed species.

Prevention & Control—Management of Canada thistle is difficult due to extensive rhizomes and often requires repeated applications of systemic herbicide. A few plant pathogens are being studied for potential use as biocontrols.

Native Alternatives—Many native plants, including native thistle species, which are important hosts for native insects.

INCISED FUMEWORT
Corydalis incisa (Thunb.) Pers. / Poppy family (Papaveraceae)

Michael Ellis

Jil Swearingen

Origin—China, Korea, Japan

Background—Incised fumewort, also known as purple keman, was first detected outside of cultivation in Bronx County, New York, in 2005. It was likely introduced as an ornamental and medicinal plant and possibly as a seed contaminant in shipped plants.

Distribution & Habitat—Incised fumewort has been reported as invasive in the District of Columbia, Maryland, New York, North Carolina, Pennsylvania, Tennessee, Virginia, and West Virginia. It is shade-tolerant and found in floodplains, streambanks, and riverbanks.

Ecological Threat—Incised fumewort emerges and reproduces in the spring and can form dense populations that threaten native spring ephemeral plant communities. Because it spreads by seed and possibly by movement of first-year tubers, it has the potential to expand rapidly and establish throughout the mid-Atlantic region.

DESCRIPTION & BIOLOGY

Plant. Incised fumewort is an annual or biennial spring ephemeral forb that grows 4–20" tall, with deeply cut leaves and showy, bilaterally symmetrical rose-purple flowers. Seeds germinate in the spring and develop small rosettes and fusiform tubers about ½" long. First-year plants die back during the summer and reemerge as rosettes that remain through the winter and produce flowering racemes in the spring.

Leaves. Alternate, stalked, and twice-pinnately compound with sharply serrate leaflets and leaf stalks 2–8" long.

Flowers, fruits & seeds. Erect racemes 1–5" tall with up to 23 tubular, rose-purple flowers, each about ½–¾" long with a floral spur. The fruit is a green capsule ½–¾" long, resembling a tiny green bean. Each capsule contains 6–12 very small elaiosome-bearing seeds that may be carried away by ants. Capsules pop open explosively when mature—throwing seeds as far as 10'—sometimes creating a seed mat on the ground.

Method of spread. Distant spread is by seeds and tubers moved by rain and flood waters and in contaminated nursery material. Local spread is through explosive dispersal of seeds and by ants attracted to the elaiosomes.

Look-alikes. Native wild bleeding-hearts (*Dicentra eximia*) with drooping pink flowers; pink corydalis (*Capnoides sempervirens*) with rose-pink flowers and yellow lips; and yellow corydalis (*Corydalis flavula*) with yellow flowers. Non-native drug fumitory (*Fumaria officinalis*) with pale lavender flowers; and spring fumewort (*Corydalis solida*) with mauve-pink, purple or white flowers.

Prevention & Control—Do not purchase or plant incised fumewort. Manual removal of mature, second-year plants can be effective. However, because the capsules are very sensitive to touch and can explode on contact, removal should be done before seed capsules mature. Removal of first-year plants is not recommended because the tubers can break off and lead to further spread.

Native Alternatives—Spring ephemerals such as yellow corydalis (*Corydalis flavula*), squirrel corn (*Dicentra canadensis*) and many other species.

MULBERRY-WEED

Fatoua villosa (Thunb.) Nakai / Mulberry family (Moraceae)

© Judy Fulton

© Judy Fulton

Origin—Australia, eastern Asia, Pacific Islands

Background—Mulberry-weed, also called hairy crabweed, is a warm-season annual first documented in Louisiana in 1964, although the species was informally reported much earlier. Initially, seeds may have come to the U.S. on repatriated military equipment after World War II and spread to greenhouses, nurseries, gardens, fields, and roadsides by hitch-hiking on landscaping products and soil. From there it readily escaped into natural areas via seed, disposal on compost piles, and dumping into woodlands. Mulberry-weed is showing up in arboreta and nurseries, possibly as a contaminant in potted plants and landscape materials.

Distribution & Habitat—Mulberry-weed is reported invasive in scattered locations from Minnesota to Texas and New York to Florida, including the District of Columbia, Maryland, and Virginia. It also occurs in California, Utah, and Washington. It prefers moist soil in part shade.

Ecological Threat—Mulberry-weed can form patches that shade out native plants and seedlings. It has the potential to spread rapidly because it can go through 2–5 flowering cycles in a year and produce a prolific amount of seed.

DESCRIPTION & BIOLOGY

Plant. An erect herbaceous plant to 2½' tall, with stems and leaves covered with velvety hairs. Lower stems are green and darken to maroon with age.

Leaves. Alternate, simple, triangular to heart-shaped with scalloped margins, usually 2–4" long by 1–2" wide with petioles about ⅔ the leaf length.

Flowers, fruits & seeds. Flowers are light green, unisexual, lack petals, and occur in densely grouped 1½–2" wide cymes that emerge from the leaf axils. Fruits are tiny, white, one-seeded achenes less than ⅒" long. A plant can start releasing seeds within 12 days of growing a second real leaf, or when only 3" tall, and continue releasing seed as it matures.

Method of spread. Distant spread is by seed transported in mulch, topsoil, yard waste, or in the soil of potted, balled, or transplanted plants. Local spread is by explosive release of seed to distances up to 4'.

Look-alikes. Native Pennsylvania pellitory (*Parietaria pensylvanica*) and clearweed (*Pilea pumila*); non-native invasive garlic mustard (*Alliaria petiolata*) and European stinging nettle (*Urtica dioica* ssp. *dioica*), and possibly the seedlings of invasive white mulberry (*Morus alba*).

Prevention & Control—Do not introduce or spread mulberry-weed. Inspect soil in and around potted plants for mulberry-weed and notify growers if it is found. Plants can be easily pulled by hand. Pulled plants should be bagged and disposed of in the trash, not placed in compost or brush piles. Eradication is difficult because mulberry-weed hides under other plants. Spreading a 3" layer of mulch on the ground has been found to decrease mulberry-weed germination by as much as ninety percent.

Native Alternatives—Red columbine (*Aquilegia Canadensis*), blue mistflower (*Conoclinum coelestinum*), wild blue phlox (*Phlox divaricata*).

FIG BUTTERCUP

Ficaria verna Huds. / Buttercup family (Ranunculaceae)

Origin—Europe

© Judy Fulton

© Judy Fulton

FORBS

Background—Fig buttercup (synonym *Ranunculus ficaria*), also known as lesser celandine and pilewort, was introduced to the U.S. as an ornamental and has spread from plantings.

Distribution & Habitat—Fig buttercup is reported invasive from Wisconsin to Texas and Vermont to Georgia, as well as in Oregon and Washington. It grows in floodplains and other moist habitats but does not tolerate permanently waterlogged conditions and does poorly in acidic and dry soils.

Ecological Threat—Fig buttercup is a spring ephemeral plant that forms extensive, dense monocultures that exclude native plants. It emerges well in advance of native spring ephemerals and poses the greatest threat to that plant community. Bare ground remaining after fig buttercup dies back may provide an opportunity for other invasive species to establish.

DESCRIPTION & BIOLOGY

Plant. Perennial that emerges in winter and reproduces in spring before dying back to the ground. Each plant produces tiny pale bulblets attached to leaf stalks and clusters of small, gray, thickened tuberous roots.

Leaves. Shiny, dark green, kidney to heart or arrow-shaped, short-stalked, with irregular wavy edges and a broad-pointed tip.

Flowers, fruits & seeds. Glossy, butter-yellow flowers with 8–12 petals, on delicate stalks that extend above the leaves; flowering occurs late winter and spring. Fruits are pubescent achenes and are uncommon.

Method of spread. Distant spread is primarily by tubers and bulblets moved by floodwaters. Local spread is by tubers and bulblets.

Look-alikes. Native marsh marigold (*Caltha palustris*), with larger, rounded, kidney-shaped, finely-toothed leaves; celandine or wood poppy (*Stylophorum diphyllum*), with twice-pinnate leaves; and the non-native invasive greater celandine (*Chelidonium majus*).

Prevention & Control—Dig up entire plants including underground tubers, bag the material and dispose of in a landfill. Systemic herbicide can be used to control plants while minimizing soil disturbance but should be timed to avoid amphibians and spring wildflowers.

Native Alternatives—Golden ragwort (*Packera aurea*) and Maryland golden-aster (*Chrysopsis mariana*).

GROUND IVY

Glechoma hederacea L. / Mint family (Lamiaceae)

© Bill Johnson

Origin—Eurasia

Background—Ground ivy, also known as gill-over-the-ground, creeping Charlie, and cat's foot, was reported in the northeastern U.S. in 1672. It has been escaping from cultivation and spreading to native plant communities since its introduction.

Distribution & Habitat—Ground ivy has been reported as invasive in natural areas in 45 states in the Lower 48. It grows in floodplains, low woods and disturbed sites, on damp, heavy, fertile, calcareous soils, and is intolerant of saline or highly acidic soils. It is also a significant weed in landscapes.

Ecological Threat—Ground ivy grows vigorously and spreads to form dense monocultures that displace and exclude native plants. As an evergreen plant, its impacts to native species are year-round.

DESCRIPTION & BIOLOGY

Plant. Perennial, low-growing, scrambling forb with square pubescent stems. Plants give off a musky mint odor when crushed.

Leaves. Opposite, kidney-shaped with scalloped (round-toothed) margins, pubescent, about 1" across.

Flowers, fruits & seeds. Flowers are about ½–¾" long, lavender, tubular, paired, and emerge from leaf axils on flowering stems that can reach 1' high. Flowering occurs from March to July. The fruit is a pod containing four smooth, tan seeds that can be long-lived in the soil.

Method of spread. Distant spread is by seed moved by rain and floodwaters. Local spread is by seed and creeping stems that root at leaf nodes.

Look-alikes. Non-native henbit (*Lamium amplexicaule*), purple deadnettle (*Lamium purpureum*) and first-year garlic mustard (*Alliaria petiolata*); native golden ragwort (*Packera aurea*) with scallop-toothed leaves.

Prevention & Control—Ground ivy is difficult to control because plants can regrow from root and stolon fragments. Plants can be hand-pulled or dug up when the soil is moist, ensuring that roots and stolons are removed. Mowing may be effective in some situations. Large infestations may need to be treated with a systemic herbicide that kills the entire plant including the roots.

Native Alternatives—Blue mistflower (*Conoclinium coelestinum*), great blue lobelia (*Lobelia siphilitica*), clustered mountain mint (*Pycnanthemum muticum*), and blue curls (*Trichostema dichotomum*).

ORANGE DAYLILY

Hemerocallis fulva (L.) L. / Asphodel family (Asphodelaceae)

© Judy Fulton

© Judy Fulton

Origin—Asia

Background—Orange daylily, also known as common daylily and tawny daylily, was introduced into the U.S. in the late 19th century as an ornamental. It is a very popular plant favored by homeowners and landscape designers for its showy flowers, hardiness, and ability to spread. There are now over 90,000 registered cultivars, many of which have the potential to become invasive and should be watched. Yellow daylily (*H. lilioasphodelus*) has also been identified as invasive in scattered locations in the eastern U.S. The buds and flowers of orange daylily are edible and have a peppery or sweet-spicy flavor.

Distribution & Habitat—Orange daylily has been reported invasive from Minnesota to Texas and Maine to Florida, and in some mid-western and western states. Daylilies prefer moist soils and full sun to partial shade. They invade fields, meadows, floodplains, moist woods and forest edges.

Ecological Threat—Daylilies multiply through tuberous roots and can form dense patches that displace native plants.

DESCRIPTION & BIOLOGY

Plant. Perennial tuberous forb, 2–4' tall with round stems.

Leaves. Bright green, linear, strap-like, 1–3' long.

Flowers, fruits & seeds. Large, with 6 tepals (3 petals and 3 sepals) and a central throat that may be the same or a different color, in clusters of up to 9 flowers, which open one per day during the summer. Fruit is a capsule.

Method of spread. Distant spread is by people improperly disposing of whole plants and by farm equipment and other machinery that uproot plants and carry them offsite. Local spread is from tuberous roots that produce new plants.

Look-alikes. Native Canada lily (*Lilium canadense*), wood lily (*L. philadelphicum*), Turk's cap lily (*L. superbum*); non-native lilyturf (*Liriope spicata*), nodding star-of-Bethlehem (*Ornithogalum nutans*), Spanish bluebells (*Hyacinthoides hispanica*).

Prevention & Control—Do not plant orange daylily or other weedy daylilies. Plants can be dug up using a shovel to remove the entire root system with tubers to prevent resprouting.

Native Alternatives—Canada lily (*Lilium canadense*), wood lily (*L. philadelphicum*), and Turk's cap lily (*L. superbum*).

DAME'S ROCKET

Hesperis matronalis L. / Mustard family (Brassicaceae)

Origin—Europe

Leslie Mehrhoff, bugwood.org

© Bill Johnson

Background—Dame's rocket, also known as dame's-violet and mother-of-the-evening, was introduced as an ornamental around the time of European settlement. It continues to be sold and used as an ornamental and is sometimes wrongly included in "native" seed mixes for homeowners.

Distribution & Habitat—Dame's rocket has been reported as invasive in natural areas in Alaska and the Lower 48 except for Texas, Louisiana, Mississippi, Georgia, Florida and South Carolina. It occurs in open woodlands, prairies, roadsides, ditches, and disturbed areas.

Ecological Threat—Dame's rocket spreads to form dense patches that displace native plants.

DESCRIPTION & BIOLOGY

Plant. Biennial forb with hairy stems. First-year plant is a rosette of leaves that remains green through the winter; second-year plant flowers in spring.

Leaves. Alternate, 2–6" long, sessile or nearly so, broadly lanceolate with toothed margins; leaves are smaller as they ascend the stem.

Flowers, fruits & seeds. Flowers are fragrant and have four white, pink or purple petals in erect, terminal clusters; flowering occurs in late spring. Fruit is a slender seed pod (silique) up to 5" long that curves upwards. Seeds are rounded, dark reddish-brown, and ripen during summer.

Method of spread. Distant spread is by seed carried by rainwater to new locations. Local spread is by abundant seed dropped by plants.

Look-alikes. Non-native annual honesty (*Lunaria annua*) with four petals; native blue phlox (*Phlox divaricata*) and fall phlox (*P. paniculata*), each with five petals.

Prevention & Control—Do not purchase or plant dame's rocket. Check native wildflower seed mixes to ensure it is not included. Plants can be pulled by hand if the soil is moist. A spade or shovel can be used to loosen the soil and help remove plants along with the entire root system. Resprouting may occur from roots left behind. A systemic herbicide may be used to kill the entire plant, including the roots.

Native Alternatives—Late figwort (*Scrophularia marilandica*), wild blue phlox (*Phlox divaricata*), fall phlox (*Phlox paniculata*), and Virginia bluebells (*Mertensia virginica*).

SERICEA LESPEDEZA

Lespedeza cuneata (Dum. Cours.) G. Don / Pea family (Fabaceae)

Wayne Longbottom

© Bill Johnson

Origin—Eastern Asia

Background—Sericea lespedeza, also called Chinese lespedeza, was introduced in the late 1800s by federal and state agencies for use in bank stabilization, erosion control, soil improvement, mine reclamation, forage, hay and other purposes. It has been escaping from plantings for many years and is a well-established invasive plant.

Distribution & Habitat—Sericea lespedeza occurs throughout much of the eastern U.S. from Minnesota to Texas, east to New York and Florida. It prefers full sun and is found in a variety of habitats including fields, prairies, floodplains, pond borders, streambanks, swamps, meadows, open woodlands, roadsides, and disturbed areas.

Ecological Threat—Sericea lespedeza poses the greatest threat to sun-adapted plant communities such as meadows, prairies, open woodlands, wetland borders and fields. It forms monocultures that displace native plants and degrade wildlife habitat by creating vegetative shelter that is too dense. The plant's high tannin content makes it unpalatable to most native animals. Sericea lespedeza develops an extensive seed bank in the soil, ensuring its long residence at a site once it has become established.

DESCRIPTION & BIOLOGY

Plant. Warm-season, perennial, upright, semi-woody forb 3–6' high with one to many slender, gray-green stems with sharp, stiff, flattened bristles and vertical lines of hairs.

Leaves. Trifoliate; each leaflet is ½–1" long, straight-sided with a wedge-shaped base and a tiny spine at the tip; lower leaf surfaces are covered with flattened hairs, giving a grayish-green appearance.

Flowers, fruits & seeds. Bilaterally symmetrical, about ¼" long, creamy white to pale yellow with purple spots at the bases of the two large upper petals; occurring singly or in clusters of 2–4 in the axils of leaves on the middle to upper parts of stems; summer. Fruits form in fall. Seeds are tiny, bean-shaped and yellow- to tan-colored.

Method of spread. Distant spread is by seed dispersed by humans, vehicles, livestock, wildlife, haying activities, and disturbances. Local spread is by seed.

Look-alikes. Native slender bush clover (*Lespedeza virginica*), non-native invasive Korean lespedeza (*Kummerowia stipulacea*) and other bush clovers.

Prevention & Control—Do not plant sericea lespedeza. Hand-pulling is impractical due to the extensive perennial root system. Mowing flowering plants as low as possible for two or three consecutive years may help to contain it. Systemic herbicides may be effective when applied in early to mid-summer.

Native Alternatives—Slender lespedeza (*Lespedeza virginica*), blue wild indigo (*Baptisia australis*), and yellow wild indigo (*Baptisia tinctoria*).

PURPLE LOOSESTRIFE

Lythrum salicaria L. / Loosestrife family (Lythraceae)

© Judy Fulton

© Bill Johnson

Origin—Eurasia

Background—Purple loosestrife was introduced to the northeastern U.S. and Canada in the 1800s for ornamental uses. It is still widely sold as an ornamental, except in states such as Minnesota, Wisconsin and Illinois, where regulations now prohibit its sale, purchase and distribution. Purple loosestrife adapts readily to natural and disturbed wetlands.

Distribution & Habitat—According to the U.S. Fish and Wildlife Service, purple loosestrife now occurs in every state except Florida. It is found in many types of wetlands, including wet freshwater meadows, tidal and non-tidal marshes, banks of rivers and streams, pond edges, reservoirs and ditches.

Ecological Threat—Purple loosestrife is able to establish rapidly and form dense stands that displace and shade out native wetland plants; suppress growth and regeneration of native plant communities; impede nesting by native birds, turtles, amphibians and other wildlife; and reduce native species biodiversity. Its dense stems and root systems trap sediment which raises water tables, reduces open waterways and restricts water flow.

DESCRIPTION & BIOLOGY

Plant. Perennial forb to 6' high with a woody rootstock and square, woody stem usually covered by downy hair. A mature plant can have 30–50 stems arising from a single rootstock and produce over 2 million seeds per year.

Leaves. Lance-shaped, stalk-less and rounded to heart-shaped at the base; arranged in pairs or whorls around the stem.

Flowers, fruits & seeds. Flowers are pink to magenta with 5–7 petals and arranged in erect terminal spikes 8–16" long; abundant nectar attracts many bee and butterfly pollinators. Flowering begins in June and continues through late summer. Fruit is a capsule containing many tiny seeds that are short-lived in the soil.

Method of spread. Distant spread is primarily by seed dispersed by wind, water, wildlife, and people. Local spread is by seed and shoots produced by underground stems.

Look-alikes. Native swamp milkweed (*Asclepias incarnata*), fireweed (*Chamerion angustifolium* ssp. *circumvagnum*), blazing star (*Liatris spicata*), Canada germander (*Teucrium canadense*), and blue vervain (*Verbena hastata*).

Prevention & Control—Do not buy or plant purple loosestrife. Young plants may be pulled by hand along with the rootstock. For small patches, spot treatment with a systemic herbicide formulated for wetland use may be effective. Biological control is an effective long-term control method for large populations of purple loosestrife and has been employed since 1992, using two European leaf beetles—*Galerucella pusilla* and *G. calmariensis*. These species were subjected to extensive testing and determined to be host specific to *Lythrum salicaria*. Although the beetles occasionally feed on other plant species, they only complete their life cycle on purple loosestrife.

Native Alternatives—Swamp milkweed (*Liatris spicata*), blazing star (*Liatris spicata*), cardinal flower (*Lobelia cardinalis*), blue vervain (*Verbena hastata*), Canada germander (*Teucrium canadense*), and ironweed (*Vernonia noveboracensis*).

MARSH DEWFLOWER

Murdannia keisak (Hassk.) Hand.-Mazz. / Spiderwort family (Commelinaceae)

Origin—Eastern Asia

Background—Marsh dewflower, also called Asian spiderwort and wart-removing herb, was first noted in 1935 in cultivated rice paddies in South Carolina. It is thought to have been introduced by accident.

Distribution & Habitat—Marsh dewflower has been reported as invasive in natural areas from Arkansas and Louisiana to New Jersey, and in Oregon and Washington. It prefers damp soil in shallow water along the edges of freshwater tidal marshes, pond margins and slow-moving streams and inhabits streambanks, canals, ditches, swamp forests, and other moist to wet disturbed places.

Jil Swearingen

Ecological Threat—Marsh dewflower forms dense mats that push out and exclude native plants. It can overtake an area fairly rapidly and form a monoculture, reducing the biodiversity and ecological value of invaded natural areas.

DESCRIPTION & BIOLOGY

Plant. Annual, creeping wetland plant with succulent stems 1–2.5' long. It grows along the soil surface, rooting at the nodes.

Leaves. Alternate, lance-shaped, up to 3" long.

Flowers, fruits & seeds. Flowers are small and solitary with three *equal-sized*, pink, lavender, or bluish-purple petals that are darker near the tip. Flowering and fruiting occur September through October. The fruit is a capsule that contains a few small seeds.

Method of spread. Distant spread is by seed consumed and dispersed by wildlife, and by root fragments moved during flood events. Local spread is by seed and new plants growing from stolons.

Look-alikes. Native Virginia dayflower (*Commelina virginica*) with 3 blue petals (2 larger, one smaller) and non-native invasive Asiatic dayflower (*Commelina communis*) with 2 large blue petals and one small white petal.

Prevention & Control—Do not purchase or plant marsh dewflower. Once established, it can be extremely difficult to control. Plants may be pulled by hand. Chemical treatment using a systemic herbicide formulated for wetland use may be somewhat effective but will need to be repeated and may damage or kill native plant species.

Native Alternatives—Virginia dayflower (*Commelina virginica*), spiderwort (*Tradescantia virginiana*), great blue lobelia (*Lobelia siphilitica*), and many other native forbs.

STAR-OF-BETHLEHEM

Nodding Star-of-Bethlehem (*Ornithogalum nutans* L.)/ Common Star-of-Bethlehem (*Ornithogalum umbellatum* L.)/ Asparagus family (Asparagaceae)

Ornithogalum nutans

Ornithogalum umbellatum

Origin—*Nodding*: Eastern and southeastern Europe, Western Asia; *Common*: Europe, western Asia, northern Africa

Background—Nodding and common star-of-Bethlehem are named for their white, star-like flowers and were introduced for ornamental purposes. Both are widely cultivated and available in the nursery trade.

Distribution & Habitat—Nodding star-of-Bethlehem has been reported as invasive in natural areas in scattered locations in the mid-Atlantic, Northeast, and Midwest, and in Oregon. Common star-of-Bethlehem has been reported invasive in 36 states in the eastern U.S., from Wisconsin to Texas and Maine to Florida, and in five western states. Both species are found in floodplains, fields, and waste places, and prefer moist soil in full sun to partial shade.

Ecological Threat—Both *Ornithogalum* species are spring ephemerals that form patches and displace native spring ephemeral plants.

DESCRIPTION & BIOLOGY

Plant. Perennial bulbiferous plant from 12" (*umbellatum*) to 20" high (*nutans*).

Leaves. Basal, linear, narrow, about ⅓–½" wide, succulent with parallel veins (*nutans*); grass-like and less than ¼" wide (*umbellatum*).

Flowers, fruits & seeds. The flower is a "perianth" consisting of 6 white or cream tepals (petal-like structures), arranged in racemes (*O. nutans*) or clusters (*O. umbellatum*), with a wide (*O. nutans*) or narrow (*O. umbellatum*) green stripe on the outside of each tepal. Fruit is an oblong-ovoid capsule with 3 sides and six ribs. Seeds are small, black, flattened and teardrop-shaped.

Method of spread. Distant and local spread is by bulbs, bulbils and seeds carried by stormwater.

Look-alikes. Native wild onion (*Allium canadense*); non-native snowdrops (*Galanthus nivalis*), summer snowflake (*Leucojum aestivum*), and white squill (*Scilla mischtschenkoana*).

Prevention & Control—Do not purchase or plant star-of-Bethlehem. Plants can be dug up with a shovel, ensuring the removal of all bulbs and bulbils to prevent regrowth.

Native Alternatives—Bloodroot (*Sanguinaria canadensis*), twinleaf (*Jeffersonia diphylla*), mayapple (*Podophyllum peltatum*), and other spring-flowering forbs.

BEEFSTEAK PLANT

Perilla frutescens (L.) Britton / Mint family (Lamiaceae)

© Judy Fulton

© Judy Fulton

Origin—Temperate and tropical Asia

Background—Also known as perilla, beefsteak plant is a traditional Asian crop used in cooking and often planted as an ornamental. It readily escapes cultivation and has become invasive in natural areas. Beefsteak plant contains chemicals that may repel herbivores and are toxic to horses and cattle, especially if cut and dried for hay late in the summer when seeds are present.

Distribution & Habitat—Beefsteak plant has been reported as invasive in natural areas from Minnesota to Texas and Massachusetts to northern Florida, and in Washington. It grows in rich, alluvial or dry soils on the banks of streams and rivers, and on gravel bars, forest edges, roadsides, railroad rights-of-way, pastures, fields and other disturbed areas.

Ecological Threat—Beefsteak plant spreads to form extensive patches that displace native plant species and reduce biodiversity.

DESCRIPTION & BIOLOGY

Plant. Annual forb to 3' high with square stems covered by short hairs. All parts of the plant emit a musky mint odor when crushed.

Leaves. Opposite, ovate, 3–4½" long by 2–3" wide, green to red-purple with serrate-toothed margins and long petioles.

Flowers, fruits & seeds. Bilaterally symmetrical with five fused petals within a calyx of five fused sepals subtended by a conspicuous ring of white hairs; red-purple; in terminal or axillary racemes. Fruits are schizocarps—dry fruits that split open into units with a single seed; seeds are tiny, round, and pale white, tan to gray. Flowering and fruiting occur late summer through fall.

Method of spread. Long distance spread is by seed dispersed by water, wind, and possibly wildlife. Local spread is by seed dropped below plants.

Look-alikes. Native citronella horse balm (*Collinsonia canadensis*) and other native mints; non-native culinary sweet basil (*Ocimum basilicum*).

Prevention & Control—Do not purchase or plant beefsteak plant. Control is possible but requires diligence. Plants can be pulled by hand, preferably prior to fruiting. Long-term monitoring is needed to look for new plants emerging from seed. If grown for culinary purposes, remove fruits to prevent spread by seed.

Native Alternatives—Spotted bee balm (*Monarda punctata*), citronella horse balm (*Collinsonia canadensis*), hyssop skullcap (*Scutellaria integrifolia*), and other native mints.

ASIAN JUMPSEED

Persicaria filiformis (Thunb.) Nakai / Smartweed family (Polygonaceae)

© Judy Fulton

© Judy Fulton

Origin—East Asia

Background—Asian jumpseed (synonyms *Polygonum filiforme* and *Tovara filiformis*) was introduced as an ornamental to the U.S. Many cultivars continue to be available from nurseries and online sources, especially 'Painter's Palette' and 'Lance Corporal'. The former is frequently planted because it has attractive variegated green and cream-colored (or very light green) leaves.

Sellers and plant enthusiasts frequently mistake this foreign interloper for a native due to a history of taxonomic confusion. Asian jumpseed was once incorrectly considered a variety of Virginia knotweed or jumpseed (*Persicaria virginiana*) and named *Persicaria virginiana* var. *filiformis* or *Polygonum virginianum* var. *filiforme*. It also does not help that the two species look similar. As a result, gardeners who think they are buying a native and being ecologically responsible can actually be spreading a highly invasive plant. To make matters worse, gardeners often share this prolific grower with their friends.

Distribution & Habitat—Asian jumpseed's distribution is uncertain due to its recent recognition as an invasive species and the confusion over its identification. This non-native has been reported in Maryland, Virginia, and the District of Columbia, and is increasingly escaping throughout the mid-Atlantic region, west to Ohio, north to Massachusetts, and to other U.S. locations. Asian jumpseed prefers to grow in part shade in very moist to medium-dry soil, in floodplains and forested uplands.

Ecological Threat—Asian jumpseed is a vigorous species that forms large, dense monocultures, which shade out native plants. Because *Persicaria* species are rarely eaten by wildlife, the invasive easily outcompetes natives more palatable to deer and other herbivores. Due to the tendency of *Persicaria* species to hybridize, Asian jumpseed could be interbreeding with, and altering the genetics of, Virginia knotweed. In natural areas, many non-variegated plants grow together with some variegated forms, along with a few of the native species.

DESCRIPTION & BIOLOGY

Plant. Perennial forb to 3½' tall, including both flowers and foliage.

Leaves. Alternate, simple leaves with a sharply pointed, dark maroon to pink or dark green chevron—an upside-down V. The chevron usually persists but can start fading towards fall. Besides the "V", a plant can have either plain green or variegated leaves. When they include whitish-cream coloring, they are offspring of 'Painter's Palette', but more often this cultivar's descendants have the non-variegated form. Plants with green leaves may also be offspring of the non-variegated 'Lance Corporal'.

Flowers, fruits & seeds. From mid-summer through early fall, very small, crimson to pink flowers bloom, spaced along thin, arching terminal spikes that extend up to 1' above the foliage. Seeds are contained in small, hooked fruits. A single plant can drop seeds to the ground nearby, or they can "jump" 10' from the stalk when touched.

Method of spread. Distant spread is by fruits attached to animal fur or carried by water. Local spread is from the many seeds propelled from each plant.

© Judy Fulton   Amanda Wray

Look-alikes. Virginia knotweed (*Persicaria virginiana* a.k.a. *Polygonum virginianum* or *Tovara virginiana*) with growth habit, height, and seed dispersal similar to Asian jumpseed, but showing a chevron with less distinct edges than the well-defined V of Asian jumpseed. This dark mark appears only on younger leaves of Virginia knotweed, and soon fades away as they mature. The chevron is especially noticeable on the first foliage of the year, but also shows in a lighter version on new growth throughout the summer. Mature leaves of Virginia jumpseed appear narrower with a more rounded base and elongate tip. Mature leaves of Asian jumpseed have a more wedge-shaped base and appear broadest closer to the tip. Virginia jumpseed almost always has greenish-white flowers compared to the Asian's reddish-pink flowers. (For the native, see rightmost leaf and flower stalk in above photos.)

Prevention & Control—To keep Asian jumpseed from becoming widely established, do not purchase it, give it away, or plant it. If you already have the invasive in your garden, pull or dig up every one of the plants, preferably before they go to seed. In natural areas, practice Early Detection and Rapid Response (EDDR) by learning how to recognize the invasive, reporting it via EDDMapS, and removing the interlopers you find. Although individual specimens are relatively easy to remove, roots and all, the plants quickly become unmanageable. The infestations that form in just a few years might require too much time and effort to control by hand. For these, a systemic herbicide might be the only option.

Native Alternatives—Virginia jumpseed (*Persicaria virginiana*).

MOCK STRAWBERRY

Potentilla indica (Andrews) Th. Wolf / Rose family (Rosaceae)

© Judy Fulton

Origin—Temperate and tropical Asia

Background—Mock strawberry synonym (*Duchesnea indica*), also known as Indian-strawberry and false strawberry, was introduced as a medicinal and ornamental plant.

Distribution & Habitat—Mock strawberry has been reported as invasive in three dozen eastern and central states, and in Colorado, California, Oregon, and Washington. It invades forests, fields, and various disturbed areas, and grows well in deep shade to full sun.

Ecological Threat—Mock strawberry spreads across the ground in forests and open habitats, forming dense continuous patches that displace native plants.

DESCRIPTION & BIOLOGY

Plant: Perennial forb with a basal rosette of leaves and long stolons that emerge from crowns and root at nodes to form new plants. Crowns produce one to several flowering stalks, each supporting a single flower.

Leaves. Compound, with three leaflets ¾–1¾" long by ½–1¼" wide, broadly ovate to obovate with blunt-toothed margins. The middle leaflet is wedge-shaped at the base; upper leaflet surfaces are hairless; leaf stalks are long and have appressed white hairs.

Flowers, fruits & seeds. Flowers are about ¾" wide with five yellow petals; the center of each flower has a pale receptacle with numerous (female) pistils surrounded by a ring of (male) stamens with yellow anthers. The petals are subtended by five long, pointed, green sepals with white ciliate margins that can be seen between the petals; the sepals are subtended by five three-toothed bracts. Flowering occurs in spring. The "strawberry" (common name for the fruit of *Fragaria*) is technically an *aggregate fruit* that develops from a single flower with more than one ovary and the ovaries join together as the fruit grows. It is spheroid or ovoid, about ½" across, red, and held erect with green sepals turned upward around it. Individual achenes (small, dry, one-seeded fruits) stick out of the fruit surface. Mock strawberry lacks flavor and has a slightly dry texture.

Method of spread. Distant spread is by small mammals and birds that eat the fruits and defecate the achenes in new locations. Local expansion is by stolons that form new crowns and by new plants growing from nodes that touch the ground.

Look-alikes. Native yellow avens (*Geum aleppicum*) and barren strawberry (*Geum fragarioides*) with five yellow flowers; wild strawberry (*Fragaria virginiana*), woodland strawberry (*F. vesca* ssp. *americana*) with five white petals; and native and non-native cinquefoils (*Potentilla*) with yellow flowers and species with three, five, seven, or more leaflets.

Prevention & Control—Plants can be pulled by hand fairly easily, especially when the ground is moist. Contact or systemic herbicides may be needed for extensive infestations.

Native Alternatives—Wild strawberry (*Fragaria virginiana*), woodland strawberry (*Fragaria vesca* ssp. *americana*), native cinquefoils (*Potentilla canadensis* and *P. simplex*), yellow avens (*Geum aleppicum*), and barren strawberry (*Geum fragarioides*).

JAPANESE KNOTWEED

Reynoutria japonica Houtt. / Buckwheat family (Polygonaceae)

© Judy Fulton

© Bill Johnson

Origin—China, Japan, Korea

Background—Japanese knotweed (synonyms *Fallopia japonica* and *Polygonum cuspidatum*) was probably introduced into the U.S. in the late 1800s as an ornamental and has also been used for erosion control. It is designated as an invasive plant in all but six states in the continental U.S. and as a noxious weed in Washington.

Distribution & Habitat—Japanese knotweed has been reported to be invasive in natural areas throughout the Continental U.S., except for Arizona, Florida, Nevada, New Mexico, North Dakota, and Texas. It can tolerate a wide variety of conditions, including deep shade, high salinity, high heat, and drought. Knotweed is commonly found near water sources, such as along streams and rivers, around old home sites, and in a variety of low-lying areas like ditches, waste places, and utility rights-of-way.

Ecological Threat—Japanese knotweed spreads quickly by strong rhizomes to form dense stands that push out and exclude native plants. It poses a significant threat to riparian areas because it can survive flooding events and rapidly colonize scoured shores and islands. It also contains allelopathic chemicals that prevent native species from growing around it. Once established, Japanese knotweed is extremely difficult to eradicate.

DESCRIPTION & BIOLOGY

Plant. Rhizomatous perennial forb that grows 4–10' tall. Stems are stout and hollow with swollen stem-leaf junctures that are surrounded by an ocrea—a membranous sheath characteristic of the buckwheat family. Plants are dioecious (i.e., male and female flowers occur on separate plants). The rhizomes are sturdy and extremely strong, enabling knotweed to penetrate the foundations of buildings into living spaces.

Leaves. Broadly oval to somewhat triangular with a truncated to heart-shaped base and a tapered tip, about 6" long and 3–4" wide.

Flowers, fruits & seeds. Very small white flowers in fingerlike inflorescences emerge from leaf axils along the entire length of the stem. Fruits are small, winged, and dangle from the flowering stems of female plants; seeds are about 1/10" long, triangular, dark brown and shiny.

Method of spread. Distant spread is by seeds, roots, and stem fragments moved in water, fill dirt, or discarded cuttings. Local spread is through seeds and growth of long, stout rhizomes.

Look-alikes. Invasive giant knotweed (*Reynoutria sachalinensis*) and its hybrid with *R. japonica*—Bohemian knotweed (*Reynoutria x bohemica*).

Prevention & Control—Do not purchase or plant invasive knotweeds including Japanese knotweed, giant knotweed or Bohemian knotweed. Control of Japanese knotweed and its invasive relatives is extremely difficult due to the ability of these species to resprout and grow from stems and rhizomes. Seedlings and younger plants can be hand-pulled or dug up when the soil is moist, ensuring removal of all roots and rhizomes. Mature flowering stems can be cut, bagged, and disposed of in a landfill. If needed, a systemic herbicide can be applied to foliage or freshly cut stems to kill the entire plant. Cutting regrowth in June to weaken the plants and then treating the new growth six to eight weeks later with a systemic herbicide can be effective. Monitoring and retreatment will be needed to control new sprouts. An insect biocontrol agent—the psyllid (*Aphalara itadori*)—was found to be suitably host-specific for Japanese knotweed, giant knotweed, and Bohemian knotweed. The USDA approved it for release in the U.S. in 2020 and it is being evaluated for efficacy at release sites in at least eight states.

Native Alternatives—Many native plants are available for restoration once Japanese knotweed has been eradicated.

EUROPEAN STINGING NETTLE
Urtica dioica L. ssp. *dioica* / Nettle family (Urticaceae)

© Bill Johnson

Jil Swearingen

Origin—Europe

Background—European stinging nettle was probably introduced to the U.S. by early immigrants for medicine, food and fiber.

Distribution & Habitat—European stinging nettle has been reported as invasive in natural areas in the mid-Atlantic in Delaware, Maryland, Pennsylvania, West Virginia, and the District of Columbia, and in New York, Georgia, Florida, California, Oregon and Washington. Its distribution is probably under-reported due to confusion with the similar-looking American stinging nettle (*Urtica dioica* ssp. *gracilis*) and over-lapping distributions and habitat preferences. Reports of stinging nettle often do not differentiate between the European and American stinging nettles. European stinging nettle invades moist floodplains, open forests, and disturbed areas.

Ecological Threat—European stinging nettle competes with and displaces native plants.

Description & Biology

Plant. Erect, perennial, dioecious (i.e., male and female flowers occur on separate plants) rhizomatous forb to 6' or higher. Stems are covered with minute, stiff, needle-like hairs that can cause a painful burning sensation lasting many hours. Stinging and non-stinging hairs can be found on stems, leaf petioles, and the undersides of the leaves, especially on veins.

Leaves. Opposite, 2–6" long, egg-shaped with heart-shaped bases and finely-toothed margins.

Flowers, fruits & seeds. Flowers are tiny, pale green to yellow, arranged in long, narrow, branched inflorescences emerging from leaf axils, and extending out horizontally or slightly drooping; May through July. Fruits form and mature July to September, producing abundant seed.

Method of spread. Distant and local spread is through underground stems (e.g., rhizomes) and rhizome fragments that are spread as a result of soil disturbance from flood events, plowing, ditch cleaning, and construction activities. Some spread may result from the movement of seeds.

Look-alikes. Native members of the nettle family including American stinging nettle (*Urtica dioica* ssp. *gracilis*), which is usually monoecious, stouter, sparsely hairy and mildly or non-stinging; alternate-leaved wood nettle (*Laportea canadensis*), false-nettle (*Boehmeria cylindrica*), and clearweed (*Pilea pumila*).

Prevention & Control—Do not plant European stinging nettle. If grown for food or medicine, ensure that it does not spread beyond the planted site by cutting and bagging flowers and fruits and pulling stray plants.

Native Alternatives—American stinging nettle (*Urtica dioica* ssp. *gracilis*), wood nettle (*Laportea canadensis*), false-nettle (*Boehmeria cylindrica*), and clearweed (*Pilea pumila*).

SHRUBS

JAPANESE ANGELICA TREE
Aralia elata (Miq.) Seem. / Ginseng family (Araliaceae)

© Judy Fulton

© Judy Fulton

Origin—China, Korea, Japan, far eastern Russian Federation

Background—Japanese angelica tree is an ornamental shrub or small tree that was introduced to the U.S. in 1830.

Distribution & Habitat—Japanese angelica tree has been reported as invasive in natural areas from Massachusetts to South Carolina, a few Great Lakes states and in Oregon and Washington. It grows in open areas, forest edges, thickets, roadsides and urban landscapes and prefers moist, well-drained loamy, sandy or clay soils in full sun to partial shade.

Ecological Threat—Japanese angelica tree grows vigorously, sprouts readily from root suckers, and can spread to form dense thickets that displace native plants. It also may hybridize with devil's walking-stick (*Aralia spinosa*), a widespread native shrub.

DESCRIPTION & BIOLOGY

Plant. A multi-stemmed deciduous shrub or small tree that can grow to 35–40' high and up to 30' across. The bark is rough, light to dark gray and has large spines spiraling around the surface.

Leaves. Alternate, large (2–4' long), twice-pinnately compound with serrate leaflets that are glaucous (waxy, whitish-green) underneath. Leaflet axils and often center veins have small spines. *Lateral veins of leaflets continue all the way*

into the marginal teeth—an important distinction from the native *Aralia spinosa*. This feature is easier to see when viewing the underside of a leaflet.

Flowers, fruits & seeds. Flowers are about ⅛" across with five white petals, arranged in a very large, *stalkless* inflorescence that emerges from the tip of the main stem. Flowering occurs July-August and the flowers are attractive to bees. Fruits are purple-black, about 1⁄10" in diameter and mature late summer to early fall (September-October). They are readily consumed by birds.

Method of spread. Distant spread is by birds that consume fruits and expel seeds in new locations. Local spread is by seed and root suckering.

Look-alikes. Native devil's walking-stick (*Aralia spinosa*), also alternate-leaved and spiny, with a very large *stalked* inflorescence that emerges from the tip of the main stem, and leaves with *lateral veins of leaflets that do not extend into the marginal teeth* (main lateral veins curve towards parallel with leaflet margins, with only smaller branching veins sometimes extending into the marginal teeth); and elderberry (*Sambucus canadensis*) with *opposite* leaves that are much smaller (6–12" long), once-pinnately compound with 5–11 leaflets, and inflorescences produced at the tips of many branches.

S H R U B S

© Judy Fulton

© Bill Johnson

Prevention & Control—Do not purchase or plant Japanese angelica tree. Be sure to correctly identify the plant before undertaking any control measures to avoid inadvertently killing native plants like devil's walking-stick and elderberry. Remove Japanese angelica tree from landscape plantings to prevent it from escaping into natural areas. Wear thick protective gloves and sturdy clothing to protect from spines. Seedlings and younger plants can be hand-pulled or dug up, ensuring that roots are completely removed. Small to medium-sized plants can be removed using a mattock, weed wrench or similar tool, preferably when the soil is moist. Inflorescences can be cut and bagged to prevent spread by birds. Large plants can be cut down and treated with a systemic herbicide applied to freshly cut surfaces to kill the entire plant, including the roots. Japanese angelica tree can regrow from small pieces of live roots and may require follow-up treatments.

Native Alternatives—Devil's walking-stick (*Aralia spinosa*), silky dogwood (*Cornus amomum*), elderberry (*Sambucus canadensis*), arrowwood viburnum (*Viburnum dentatum*).

JAPANESE BARBERRY

Berberis thunbergii DC. / Barberry family (Berberidaceae)

Leslie Mehrhoff, bugwood.org

Leslie Mehrhoff, bugwood.org

Origin—Japan

Background—Japanese barberry was introduced to the U.S. as an ornamental in 1875, when seeds were sent from Russia to the Arnold Arboretum in Boston, Massachusetts. In 1896, Japanese barberry was planted at the New York Botanic Garden, where it was grown and cultivated for horticultural uses. Japanese barberry was eventually promoted as a substitute for common barberry (*Berberis vulgaris*)—a related non-native invasive shrub that was introduced from Europe by early settlers and later found to be a host for black stem rust, a serious disease of wheat. Japanese barberry is resistant to the rust and is hybridizing with common barberry to create the hybrid *B.* x *ottawensis*. Offspring of the hybrid are capable of producing rust-susceptible hybrids. Black stem rust could pose a threat to native barberry species (e.g., *B. canadensis*, which is absent from, or rare in, much of the mid-Atlantic).

Distribution & Habitat—Japanese barberry has been reported as invasive in natural areas from Minnesota to Kansas and Maine to Georgia, and in Washington and Wyoming. It grows in a variety of habitats from closed canopy forests to open

© Judy Fulton   Leslie Mehrhoff, bugwood.org

woodlands, fields, wetlands, and disturbed lands, and tolerates full sun to deep shade.

Ecological Threat—Japanese barberry forms dense stands of deep shade and produces extensive fine-root biomass in the soil surface layer that displaces and excludes native plants. Breakdown of the leaves increases the pH of the soil, making it more basic and less favorable for most native plants. According to Williams et al. 2017, the shrub's dense growth creates a moist, shady microhabitat that favors high populations of the black-legged tick (*Ixodes scapularis*)—carrier of *Borrelia burgdorferi*, the bacterium that causes Lyme disease.

DESCRIPTION & BIOLOGY

Plant. Deciduous shrub from 3–6' high with brown, deeply-grooved, zig-zag branches, simple to 3-pronged spines, and yellow inner bark.

Leaves. Small (½–1½" long), paddle-shaped with a tapering leaf base and smooth margins. Leaf color ranges from green to yellow and crimson.

Flowers, fruits & seeds. Abundant cream to pale yellow axillary flowers occur singly or in clusters of 2–5 along the entire length of the stem in spring. Fruits are bright red, dry-fleshed berries, about ⅓" long that dangle from stems, mature July to October and persist through the winter. Seeds are produced in large quantities; most germinate the first year but some can survive in the soil for two years.

Method of spread. Distant spread is by turkey, grouse, and other wildlife that eat the fruits and defecate seeds in new locations. Local spread is by creeping roots, tip-rooting branches, and sprouts from rhizomes.

Look-alikes. Native American barberry (*Berberis canadensis*) with brown, purple, or reddish second-year branches, leaf margins with teeth alternating with smooth edges (unlike the completely smooth margins of *B. thunbergii*), and inflorescences with a few yellow flowers. Non-native and invasive common barberry (*Berberis vulgaris*) and wintergreen barberry (*B. julianae*), with 3-pronged spines, and either drooping, axillary clusters of very small (less than ¼" wide) yellow flowers in 1–2" long panicles (*B. vulgaris*) or drooping rounded clusters of yellow flowers (*B. julianae*).

Prevention & Control—Do not purchase or plant Japanese barberry or other non-native barberries. Remove Japanese barberry from landscapes to prevent spread into natural areas. Wear thick protective gloves and sturdy clothing to protect from spines. Hand-pull or dig up young plants, ensuring complete removal of roots and rhizomes. Larger plants can be removed using a mattock, weed wrench or similar tool, preferably when the soil is moist. If necessary, plants can be cut down and treated with a systemic herbicide applied to freshly cut stems to kill the entire plant, including the roots. Because barberry can regrow from roots and rhizomes, it needs to be completely removed and monitored for regrowth.

Native Alternatives—Winterberry (*Ilex verticillata*), smooth winterberry (*Ilex laevigata*), inkberry (*Ilex glabra*), American strawberry bush (*Euonymus americanus*), red chokeberry (*Aronia arbutifolia*).

AUTUMN-OLIVE

Elaeagnus umbellata Thunb. / Oleaster family (Elaeagnaceae)

Origin—East Asia

Leslie Mehrhoff, bugwood.org

Leslie Mehrhoff, bugwood.org

Background—Autumn-olive was introduced into the U.S. in 1830 and widely planted for over a century for ornamental purposes, mine reclamation, degraded land restoration, erosion control, windbreaks, and wildlife habitat. By 1954, it had been declared a noxious weed in 43 states. The only native species of *Elaeagnus* in the U.S. is silverberry (*Elaeagnus commutata*), which ranges from Minnesota to Utah.

Distribution & Habitat—Autumn-olive has been reported as invasive in natural areas from Minnesota to Louisiana and Maine to Florida, and in Kansas, Montana, Nebraska, Oregon and Washington. It grows best on deep, relatively coarse-textured, moderately to well-drained soils, and invades grasslands, fields, open woodlands and various disturbed areas. Autumn-olive forms root nodules as a result of symbiosis with actinomycetes fungi in the soil—an association that allows it to fix and use atmospheric nitrogen and grow on bare mineral substrates.

Ecological Threat—Autumn-olive forms dense impenetrable thickets that push out native plants, impede natural plant community succession, and disrupt nutrient cycling.

DESCRIPTION & BIOLOGY

Plant. Deciduous, multi-branched, thorny shrub 10–16' high with stems, buds and leaves covered by silvery to rusty-colored scales.

Leaves. Alternate, deciduous, egg- or lance-shaped with smooth margins, dull green upper leaf surfaces and lower leaf surfaces covered with silvery to brown scales.

Flowers, fruits & seeds. Flowers are white to pale yellow, fused at the base with four pointed-tip petals; June-July. Flowers have a distinctive sweet-musky aroma and are insect-pollinated. Fruits are round, red, *juicy* single-seeded drupes flecked with tiny silvery to brown scales, in abundant dense clusters along the stems; August to November.

Method of spread. Distant spread is by fruit-eating birds and some small mammals that defecate the seeds in new locations.

Look-alikes. Non-native invasive **Russian-olive** (*Elaeagnus angustifolia*) with narrow-elongate leaves covered with silvery scales on both upper and lower surfaces, and yellow or silvery, mealy fruit; and **thorny-olive** (*E. pungens*) with oval to elliptical evergreen leaves with wavy margins that are shiny green above and silvery below.

Prevention & Control—Do not purchase or plant any *Elaeagnus* in the mid-Atlantic region. Young plants and seedlings can be hand-pulled or dug up, removing all roots. Larger plants can be removed using a mattock, weed wrench or similar tool. Cutting, mowing and burning will result in vigorous resprouting. However, cutting plants down and treating freshly cut surfaces with a systemic herbicide can be very effective. Canker disease may weaken autumn-olive.

Native Alternatives—Winterberry (*Ilex verticillata*), downy serviceberry (*Amelanchier arborea*), red chokeberry (*Aronia arbutifolia*), black chokeberry (*A. melanocarpa*), northern bayberry (*Morella pensylvanica*).

WINGED BURNING BUSH

Euonymus alatus (Thunb.) Siebold / Bittersweet family (Celastraceae)

© Bill Johnson   © Judy Fulton

Origin—Northeastern Asia, Japan, Central China

Background—Winged burning bush, also known as winged euonymus, winged wahoo, and winged spindle, was introduced to the U.S. around 1860 as an ornamental. Despite its invasive nature, it remains very popular and is widely sold for its hardiness and intense red fall foliage. It is ubiquitous and can be found planted along roadways, at commercial and industrial sites, and in park and residential landscapes.

Distribution & Habitat—Winged burning bush has been reported as invasive from Minnesota to Louisiana and Maine to Georgia and in scattered locations in Kansas, Colorado, Oklahoma and Montana. It grows in forests, floodplains, coastal scrublands, grasslands, and disturbed habitats and prefers moist, well-drained soils in full sun or part shade. It can tolerate full shade, wet soils, and drought.

Ecological Threat—Winged burning bush forms dense thickets, displacing many native woody and herbaceous plant species. Hundreds of seedlings are often found below the parent plant in its "seed shadow."

© Judy Fulton   © Bill Johnson

DESCRIPTION & BIOLOGY

Plant. Multiple-stemmed, angular branching shrub 5–20' high with winged stems except on young plants.

Leaves. Deciduous, opposite, dark green, turning brilliant red-purple in fall.

Flowers, fruits & seeds. Inconspicuous, greenish flowers occur in late spring, and red-purple fruits mature during summer.

Method of spread. Distant spread is by fruit-eating birds that expel the seeds in new locations. Local spread is by seed.

Look-alikes. Non-native and invasive Japanese euonymus (*Euonymus japonicus*) and European spindle (*Euonymus europaeus*); native American strawberry bush (*Euonymus americanus*), eastern wahoo (*Euonymus atropurpureus*), winged sumac (*Rhus copallinum*), and saplings of native sweetgum (*Liquidambar styraciflua*) with winged trunks and branches.

Prevention & Control—Do not purchase or plant winged burning bush or any other non-native *Euonymus*. Young plants can be pulled by hand. Larger plants can be dug up with a shovel or removed using a weed wrench type tool, when the soil is moist, to help remove the roots and prevent sprouting from the root crown. Shrubs can also be cut down and treated with a systemic herbicide applied to freshly cut surfaces to kill the entire plant, including the roots.

Native Alternatives—American strawberry bush (*Euonymus americanus*), Eastern wahoo (*Euonymus atropurpureus*), and winged sumac (*Rhus copallinum*).

SHRUBS

PRIVET

Border privet (*Ligustrum obtusifolium* Siebold & Zucc.) / **Garden privet** (*Ligustrum ovalifolium* Hassk.) / **Chinese privet** (*Ligustrum sinense* Lour.) / **European privet** (*Ligustrum vulgare* L.) / **Olive family (Oleaceae)**

© Bill Johnson

Leslie Mehrhoff, bugwood.org

Origin—**Border privet**: Japan; **garden privet**: Japan, South Korea; **Chinese privet**: China; **European privet**: Europe, Morocco, western Asia, Caucasus

Background—There are no U.S. native privets (*Ligustrum*). Since the 1800s, eight or nine privet species have been introduced to the U.S. as ornamental plants. They are commonly used as hedges in gardens and landscapes, from which they escape, and are estimated to be invading over a million acres of natural habitat.

Distribution & Habitat—The four privet species featured here have been reported as invasive in natural areas in varying locations in the Lower 48. **Border privet** is more common in the northeastern states; **garden privet** is in scattered locations in the eastern U.S. and a few western states; **Chinese privet** is very common in the Southeast and mid-Atlantic states; and **European privet** is in scattered locations in the Northeast, Midwest, and Pacific Northwest. Other introduced privets, including **Amur privet** (*L. obtusifolium* ssp. suave), **Japanese privet** (*L. japonicum*), **glossy privet** (*L. lucidum*), and **waxyleaf privet** (*L. quihoui*), have also been reported as invasive in natural areas the U.S. including the mid-Atlantic region. Privets grow in barrens, glades, floodplains, fields, forests, forest edges, and riparian areas and prefer moist soils.

Ecological Threat—Privets form dense thickets that shade and crowd out native shrubs and forbs. The leaves of privet contain phenolic compounds that make them *unpalatable to native leaf-feeding insects*. As a result, caterpillars and other herbivorous insects that serve as bird food avoid feeding on privet leaves.

Jil Swearingen　　　　　　　　　　　　*Leslie Mehrhoff, bugwood.org*

Privet fruit is somewhat important to native cedar waxwings and bobwhite quail that eat the drupes in winter when other fruit sources may be less available.

DESCRIPTION & BIOLOGY

Plant. Deciduous or semi-evergreen shrubs that grow 8–20' high. Presence or absence of hairs and type of hairs on stems are helpful in distinguishing species. The branchlets of **garden** privet are smooth and usually shiny; **border**, **Chinese**, and **European** privet branchlets have small hairs.

Leaves. Opposite, simple, entire, short-stalked, 1–2 ⅓" long, and oval, elliptic, or oblong. Chinese privet leaves are 1–1 ⅕" long; garden, border and European privet leaves are 1–2 ⅓" long.

Flowers, fruits & seeds. Flowers are small, fragrant, white and tubular with four petals, and occur in clusters at branch tips from May to July. Corolla tube lengths range from a maximum of ⅒" for Chinese and common privet and up to ⅓" for garden and European privet. The fruit is a small black to blue-black oval to spherical drupe (i.e., a fleshy fruit with one to several stony seeds inside) and matures late summer to fall. A single plant can produce hundreds of fruits.

Method of spread. Distant spread is by birds that consume fruits and excrete seeds in new locations. Local spread is by seed and through root sprouting.

Look-alikes. Native and non-native woody plants with opposite, entire leaves (e.g., *Cornus*, *Lonicera*, *Viburnum*).

Prevention & Control—Do not plant privets; all *Ligustrum* are non-native. Remove privets from ornamental landscapes and natural areas, and cut and bag fruits to prevent spread by birds. Hand-pull or dig up seedlings and younger plants, ensuring that the roots are completely removed. Remove mature plants using a mattock, weed wrench or similar tool. Large plants can also be cut and treated with a systemic herbicide applied to freshly cut surfaces to kill the entire plant, including the roots. A leaf-feeding insect native to Europe (*Macrophya punctumalbum*), a fungal leaf spot (*Pseudocercospora ligustri*), and a common root crown bacteria (*Agrobacterium tumefaciens*) affect privets to some extent.

Native Alternatives—Inkberry (*Ilex glabra*), winterberry (*Ilex verticillata*), red chokeberry (*Aronia arbutifolia*), black chokeberry (*Aronia melanocarpa*), and native viburnums including blackhaw (*Viburnum prunifolium*).

AMUR HONEYSUCKLE
Lonicera maackii (Rupr.) Maxim. / Honeysuckle family (Caprifoliaceae)

© Bill Johnson   © Judy Fulton

Origin—China, Japan, Korea, Russian Far East

Background—Amur honeysuckle is an ornamental shrub that was imported in 1898 through the New York Botanical Garden. It has been widely planted for wildlife cover and for soil erosion control, and has been escaping from plantings into natural areas for many decades. Other non-native invasive shrub honeysuckles include **fragrant honeysuckle** (*L. fragrantissima*), **Standish's honeysuckle** (*L. standishii*), **European fly honeysuckle** (*L. xylosteum*), **Morrow's honeysuckle** (*L. morrowii*), **Tatarian honeysuckle** (*L. tatarica*) and **Bell's honeysuckle** (*L.* x *bella*)—a hybrid of *L. morrowii* and *L. tatarica*.

Distribution & Habitat—Amur honeysuckle has been reported as invasive in natural areas from Wisconsin to Texas and Maine to Georgia. It occurs in disturbed habitats including forest edges and interiors, floodplains, old fields, pastures, and roadsides. It grows especially well on calcareous soils in full sun to deep shade.

Ecological Threat—Amur honeysuckle forms dense thickets that shade out native plants and interfere with restoration of forests and native plant communities. It produces allelopathic chemicals that suppress native plant and associated mycorrhizal fungi (Miller et al. 2004; Shannon et al. 2014), accelerate leaf litter decomposition, and increase carbon and nitrogen in the soil (Kolbe et al. 2015). Its branching structure facilitates nest access by snakes and other predators resulting in reduced brood success rates for cardinals, robins and other bird species (Schmidt et al. 1999). Unlike the lipid-rich fruits of many native plants that sustain migrating bird species, Amur honeysuckle berries are high in carbohydrates (Smith et al. 2013). Chemical toxins in Amur honeysuckle negatively affect native insects (Cipollini et al. 2008) and can kill or cause behavioral changes in young amphibians (Watling et al. 2011). It also increases mammalian susceptibility to illness from *Ehrlichia* bacteria transmitted by the lone star tick, *Amblyomma americanum* (Allan et al. 2010).

DESCRIPTION & BIOLOGY

Plant. Deciduous shrub to 20' high. Pith of mature stems is **hollow** and white or tan, in contrast to the **solid** white pith of native shrub honeysuckle species.

Leaves. Opposite, entire, about 1 ½–3 ¾" long, ovate, slightly pubescent, with long tapering tip.

Flowers, fruits & seeds. Flowers are tubular, less than 1" long, with five petals (the upper 4 are fused), white to pinkish, fading to yellow, and in pairs borne from the leaf axils. Flowering occurs May-June. Fruits are red to orange-red, paired, many-seeded berries that mature in late summer and persist through the winter.

Method of spread. Distant spread is by birds that consume fruits and expel seeds in new locations. Local spread is by seed and vegetative sprouting.

Look-alikes. Non-native invasive Morrow's honeysuckle (*Lonicera morrowii*), Tatarian honeysuckle (*L. tatarica*) and Standish's honeysuckle (*L. standishii*). Native Northern bush honeysuckle (*Diervilla lonicera*) with toothed leaves; mountain fly honeysuckle (*Lonicera caerulea* var. *villosa*) with elliptic to ovate, glaucous green leaves and an edible blueberry-like fruit; and smooth or limber honeysuckle (*L. dioica*), a low-climbing, vine-like shrub with short red flowers emerging from a pair of fused leaves at the stem tip.

Prevention & Control—Do not purchase or plant Amur honeysuckle or other non-native bush honeysuckles. Remove shrubs from ornamental landscapes and natural areas and cut and bag fruits to prevent spread by birds. Hand-pull or dig up seedlings and younger plants, ensuring that the roots are completely removed. Large plants can be extracted using a mattock, weed wrench or similar tool, or cut and treated with a systemic herbicide to kill the entire plant, including the roots.

Native Alternatives—Northern bush honeysuckle (*Diervilla lonicera*), smooth winterberry (*Ilex laevigata*), and arrowwod viburnum (*Viburnum dentatum*).

MORROW'S HONEYSUCKLE

Lonicera morrowii A. Gray / Honeysuckle family (Caprifoliaceae)

© Bill Johnson   © Judy Fulton

Origin—Japan, South Korea

Background—Morrow's honeysuckle was imported in the 1800s as an ornamental, for wildlife food and cover, and for soil erosion control. It was widely planted throughout the 20th century and is a highly invasive species impacting natural areas as well as managed parks, gardens and other lands.

Distribution & Habitat—Morrow's honeysuckle has been reported as invasive from Minnesota to Oklahoma and Maine to Georgia, and in Oklahoma, Montana, Wyoming, Colorado and New Mexico. It invades forest edges, open woodlands, floodplains, pastures, old fields, roadsides and other disturbed areas and is shade-tolerant.

Ecological Threat—Morrow's honeysuckle forms dense thickets, and outcompetes and displaces native shrubs, trees and herbaceous plants. Its dense growth can impede reforestation efforts. With a branching structure very similar to that of Amur honeysuckle, Morrow's honeysuckle likely also encourages increased nest predation (Schmidt, et al.). Like Amur honeysuckle and other non-native *Lonicera*, the fruits are carbohydrate-rich and cannot sustain migratory birds on long-distant flights (Smith et al.).

DESCRIPTION & BIOLOGY

Plant. Deciduous shrub to 8' high. The pith of mature stems is *hollow* in contrast to the *solid* white pith of native shrub honeysuckle species.

Leaves. Opposite, entire, ¾–2" long, elliptic to oblong, sharp-pointed tip, short-stalked, with soft grayish pubescence on lower side.

Flowers, fruits & seeds. Flowers are paired, axillary, fused or tubular at the base with five white, narrow, separate petals. Fruits are paired, red to orange, many-seeded berries that mature in July and persist through winter.

Method of spread. Distant spread is by birds that eat the fruits and expel the seeds in new locations. Local spread is by seed and vegetative sprouting.

Look-alikes. Non-native invasive Amur honeysuckle (*Lonicera maackii*), Tatarian honeysuckle (*L. tatarica*) and Standish's honeysuckle (*L. standishii*). Native Northern bush honeysuckle (*Diervilla lonicera*) with toothed leaves; smooth or limber honeysuckle (*Lonicera dioica*), a low-climbing, vine-like shrub with red or yellow flowers emerging from a pair of fused leaves at the stem tip.

SHRUBS

Prevention & Control—Do not purchase or plant Morrow's honeysuckle or any other non-native bush honeysuckle. Remove shrubs from ornamental landscapes and natural areas to prevent spread by birds. Hand-pull or dig up seedlings and younger plants, ensuring that the roots are completely removed. Large plants can be removed using a mattock, weed wrench or similar tool. If needed, large plants can be cut and treated with a systemic herbicide to kill the entire plant, including the roots.

Native Alternatives—Northern bush honeysuckle (*Diervilla lonicera*), smooth winterberry (*Ilex laevigata*), and arrowwod viburnum (*Viburnum dentatum*).

LEATHERLEAF MAHONIA

Mahonia bealei (Fortune) Carrière / Barberry family (Berberidaceae)

© Judy Fulton

© Judy Fulton

Origin—China

Background—Leatherleaf mahonia (synonym *Berberis bealei*), also known as Beale's barberry and holly-grape, was introduced as an ornamental, possibly as early as the 1800s. It escapes from plantings and invades natural areas.

Distribution & Habitat—Leatherleaf mahonia has been reported as invasive in natural areas in scattered locations from Illinois to Mississippi and Delaware to Florida. It grows in full sun to deep shade and is found in moist, well-drained, acidic to basic, clay, loam and sandy soils.

Ecological Threat—Leatherleaf mahonia's large leathery leaves and spreading nature create deep shade that pushes out native plants. Deer and other animals avoid the plant's tough, spiny foliage.

DESCRIPTION & BIOLOGY

Plant. Evergreen shrub to 10' high and 6' wide with thick, upright stems of holly-like leaflets. The chemical berberine gives plant parts a deep yellow color.

Leaves. Alternate, evergreen, pinnately-compound with paired, sessile leaflets, a single, larger terminal leaflet and a reddish leaf stalk. Leaflets are glossy, leathery, and holly-like with long spines protruding from the margins.

Flowers, fruits & seeds. Flowers are bright yellow, bell-shaped, stalked, in upright arching racemes that emerge from branch tips in late winter to early spring. The fruit is an oval, green to bluish-purple berry with a waxy grayish bloom that hangs in elongated clusters.

Method of spread. Distant spread is by birds that consume the fruits and expel the seeds in new locations. Local spread is by seed.

Look-alikes. Non-native Japanese mahonia (*Mahonia japonica*), and Oregon-grape (*Mahonia aquifolium*) which is native to California, Idaho, Montana, Oregon and Washington and should not be planted outside its native range (e.g., in the eastern U.S.) because it could become invasive.

Prevention & Control—Do not buy or plant leatherleaf mahonia. Remove it from ornamental landscapes and natural areas, and cut and bag fruits to prevent spread by birds. Wearing thick gloves to protect skin from the sharp spines, hand-pull or dig up seedlings and younger plants, ensuring that the roots are completely removed. Mature plants can be removed using a mattock, weed wrench or similar tool. If needed, plants can be cut down and treated with a systemic herbicide applied to freshly cut stems to kill the entire plant, including the roots. Cutting alone is not an effective control because leatherleaf mahonia resprouts vigorously.

Native Alternatives—Evergreen shrubs like inkberry (*Ilex glabra*) and mountain laurel (*Kalmia latifolia*).

MULTIFLORA ROSE

Rosa multiflora Thunb. / Rose family (Rosaceae)

Jil Swearingen

© Judy Fulton

Origin—Japan, Korea, Eastern China

Background—Multiflora rose was introduced to the eastern U.S. in 1866 as rootstock for ornamental roses. Beginning in the 1930s, the Soil Conservation Service promoted it for erosion control and as a "living fence" for livestock. State conservation departments recommended multiflora rose as cover for wildlife and planted it widely. Its tenacious growth was eventually recognized as a problem

© Judy Fulton

Leslie Mehrhoff, bugwood.org

on pastures and unplowed lands, where it disrupted cattle grazing, and, more recently, as a pest of natural ecosystems. Multiflora rose is designated a noxious weed in Iowa, Ohio, New Jersey, Pennsylvania and West Virginia.

Distribution & Habitat—Multiflora rose is reported as invasive in natural areas from Minnesota to Texas and Maine to Florida, and in scattered locations in western states. It invades fields, forests, prairies, some wetlands, and many other habitats, and tolerates a wide range of soil, moisture and light conditions.

Ecological Threat—Multiflora rose grows vigorously, forming dense, prickly thickets that displace and shade out native plants.

DESCRIPTION & BIOLOGY

Plant. Multi-stemmed shrub and climbing vine, with arching stems and sharp, curved prickles that catch in fur and rip skin.

Leaves. Alternate, pinnately compound, with 5–11 sharply-toothed leaflets and paired, fringed "eyelash-like" stipules at the base of the leaf stalk, which are an important identifying feature.

Flowers, fruits & seeds. White (sometimes pink or red), about 1" wide, with five broad petals, in clusters of pyramid-shaped, many-flowered panicles. Flowering occurs in May. Large numbers of ¼–½" long bright red fruits (rose-hips) develop during the summer and remain through the winter. An average plant can produce a million seeds per year that remain viable in the soil for up to 20 years.

Method of spread. Distant spread is by seed consumed by birds and mammals and expelled in new locations. Local spread is through seed and vegetative sprouting of new plants from the tips of arching canes that root where they contact the ground.

Look-alikes. Native pasture rose (*Rosa carolina*), swamp rose (*Rosa palustris*), Allegheny blackberry (*Rubus allegheniensis*), and flowering raspberry (*Rubus odoratus*). Only multiflora rose has the combination of upright arching stems and fringed, eyelash-like stipules.

Prevention & Control—Do not plant multiflora rose. Wear thick gloves and tough clothing to protect from the painful prickles. Seedlings and young plants can be hand-pulled or dug up, ensuring that the roots are completely removed. Large plants can be cut back and removed using a mattock, weed wrench or similar tool. Frequent cutting or mowing, up to 3–6 times per growing season and repeated for 2–4 years can be very effective. Because the seed remains viable in the soil for many years, follow-up treatments are usually necessary. Plants can also be treated with a systemic herbicide, which is usually more effective later in the growing season. Goats can be employed to consume above-ground plant parts. Two naturally occurring biological controls affect multiflora rose. Rose-rosette disease, caused by a native virus (Emaravirus) that is spread by a native eriophyid mite (*Phyllocoptes fructiphylus*), impedes stem growth and can kill a shrub within three years. European rose chalcid (*Megastigmus aculeatus*) is an introduced seed-infesting wasp that may help reduce the plant's spread.

Native Alternatives—Pasture rose (*Rosa carolina*), swamp rose (*Rosa palustris*).

WINEBERRY

Rubus phoenicolasius Maxim. / Rose family (Rosaceae)

Origin—Japan, Korea, China

© Judy Fulton

Jil Swearingen

Background—Wineberry, also known as wine raspberry, was introduced into the U.S. in 1890 as breeding stock for new raspberry cultivars and is still used today by berry breeders. Despite its well-known invasive tendencies, wineberry is often planted and maintained for its tasty, raspberry-like fruit.

Distribution & Habitat—Wineberry has been reported as invasive in natural areas from Illinois to Arkansas and Vermont to Georgia, and in California. It prefers moist habitats and occurs in forests, fields, streams, wetland edges, and open woods.

Ecological Threat—Wineberry forms dense shady thickets that alter habitat conditions and displace native plants.

DESCRIPTION & BIOLOGY

Plant. Multi-stemmed shrub to 6' high. Stems (canes) and inflorescences are densely covered with reddish, or sometimes greenish, gland-tipped hairs and scattered, straight, slender prickles.

Leaves. Alternate, compound, with three leaflets: a pair of basal leaflets and a much larger terminal leaflet. Leaf surfaces are green above, densely white below, and coarsely toothed.

Flowers, fruits & seeds. Flowers are small, about ¼" wide, with five white petals surrounded by five much larger, glandular-hairy sepals that are conspicuous on the buds. Flowers are arranged in many-flowered panicles and occur in spring. Fruits are bright red, raspberry-like berries produced in early summer.

Method of spread. Distant spread is by birds and mammals that eat the fruit and expel the seeds in new locations. Local spread is by seed and by new plants sprouting from root buds or from tips of canes that touch the ground.

Look-alikes. Native and non-native raspberries and blackberries (*Rubus*), native roses (*Rosa*), and non-native invasive multiflora rose (*Rosa multiflora*): all lack the combination of *fuzzy red or green glandular hairs and 3 leaflets with white tomentose undersides.*

Prevention & Control—Do not purchase or plant wineberry. Hand-pull or dig up seedlings and younger plants, ensuring that the roots are completely removed. Larger plants can be extracted using a weed wrench or similar tool. Wear thick gloves to protect from the prickles. Mature plants can also be cut to the ground and treated with a systemic herbicide applied to freshly cut stems to kill the entire plant, including the roots.

Native Alternatives—Black raspberry (*Rubus occidentalis*), purple-flowering raspberry (*Rubus odoratus*), Pennsylvania blackberry (*Rubus pensilvanicus*).

JAPANESE MEADOWSWEET

Spiraea japonica L. f. / Rose family (Rosaceae)

© Judy Fulton

© Judy Fulton

Origin—Japan, Korea, China

Background—Japanese meadowsweet, also known as Japanese spiraea, was introduced into the U.S. around 1870 to 1880 as an ornamental due to its showy rosy-pink to carmine flowers. It continues to be a popular garden plant today.

Distribution & Habitat—Japanese meadowsweet has been reported as invasive in natural areas from Minnesota to Louisiana and Maine to Georgia. It tolerates a wide range of soil and light conditions and grows in forest interiors, forest edges, riparian areas, roadsides, powerline rights-of-way, and various disturbed areas.

Ecological Threat—Japanese meadowsweet can form dense patches that fill in open areas and create deep shade that displaces native woody and herbaceous plants and impedes growth of native seedlings.

DESCRIPTION & BIOLOGY

Plant. Deciduous shrub, 4–6' tall, with brown to red-brown stems.

Leaves. Alternate, oval to lance-shaped, 3–6" long with coarsely toothed margins, dark green above with pubescent veins on the leaf underside.

Flowers, fruits & seeds. Flowers are small, about ¼" across, pink or rarely white, produced at branch tips and arranged in dense, slightly rounded clusters with progressively shorter inner central flower stalks. Flowering occurs July-August. Fruit is a dry brown capsule (an aggregate of follicles) that matures in fall. Once the follicles split open, the capsules form an attractive star-like structure. Seeds are very small, dry, tan, elongate, wedge-shaped, and flattened.

Method of spread. Spread is by seed, produced in abundance and dropped near the parent plant. It can be moved to distant locations by rain water and in fill-dirt.

Look-alikes. Native white meadowsweet (*Spiraea alba*) with white flowers in narrow branched clusters; non-native and invasive Thunberg's meadowsweet (*Spiraea thunbergii*) and bridal-wreath spiraea (*Spiraea prunifolia*).

Prevention & Control—Do not purchase or plant Japanese meadowsweet. Hand-pull or dig up seedlings and younger plants, ensuring that the roots are completely removed. Remove larger plants using a weed wrench or similar tool. Mature plants can also be cut to the ground and treated with a systemic herbicide to kill the entire plant, including the roots. Repeated mowing or cutting will control the spread of spiraea to some extent, but will not eradicate it.

Native Alternatives—White meadowsweet (*Spiraea alba*), ninebark (*Physocarpus opulifolius*), sweet pepperbush (*Clethra alnifolia*), silky dogwood (*Cornus amomum*), Virginia sweetspire (*Itea virginica*), leatherleaf (*Dirca palustris*).

ASIAN VIBURNUMS

Linden Viburnum (*Viburnum dilatatum* Thunb.) / Japanese snowball (*Viburnum plicatum* Thunb.) / Doublefile Viburnum (*Viburnum plicatum* var. *tomentosum* Miq.) / Tea Viburnum (*Viburnum setigerum* Hance) / Siebold Viburnum (*Viburnum sieboldii* Miq.) / Viburnum family (Viburnaceae)

Origin—China, Japan, Korea, Taiwan

© Bill Johnson

© Bill Johnson

Background—Ornamental, non-native viburnums were introduced for cultivated landscapes starting in the early 1800s and are popular garden plants.

Distribution & Habitat—Linden, Japanese snowball/doublefile, tea and Siebold viburnums have been reported as invasive in natural areas from Massachusetts and Michigan south to North Carolina and Missouri, as well as in Oregon. Although Linden and Siebold viburnums might predominate, it is difficult to determine the accuracy of sightings because of similarities in appearance. These five species grow in disturbed and undisturbed forests, forest edges, and old fields, in full sun to part shade, and in mesic conditions.

Ecological Threat—Invasive viburnums can form thickets that cast deep shade, suppressing native plants. A dense cover of young plants produced from seed and vegetative regrowth can cover the ground in infested areas. These non-native viburnums leaf out earlier in the spring and keep their leaves later into the fall than most native plants, giving them a competitive advantage over natives. Deer further assist in the spread of these invasive shrubs by preferentially feeding on native viburnums.

DESCRIPTION & BIOLOGY

Plant. Linden, Japanese snowball/doublefile, tea and Siebold viburnums are multi-stemmed, deciduous shrubs with opposite leaves and branches. These species can be difficult to differentiate due to their very similar appearances. All have upright to rounded forms that spread out to be almost as wide as tall, but multiple plants can grow next to each other to cover much more ground. Depending on the species, they can grow from 8–20' high with a dense habit. To differentiate among them, use an accurate and detailed key, such as *Flora of Virginia*, Alan Weakley's *Flora of the Southeastern United States*, or Cornell University's *Guide to identifying viburnums*.

Leaves. Opposite, simple, unlobed, with toothed margins and a ribbed appearance due to strong venation. Leaves vary from rounder to more oblong depending on the species, individual plant or even individual leaf. Unreliable fall color can be red, purple, rust or brown.

Flowers, fruits & seeds. Many small creamy white flowers in numerous flattened clusters. Tea viburnum has clusters 1–2" wide, and the other four species flower clusters 3–6" wide. Flowers bloom in mid to late spring. The fruits are attractive, vividly colored, oval, clustered drupes. Linden viburnum has red fruit, tea viburnum has red to orange fruit, and Siebold and Japanese snowball/doublefile viburnums have red fruit that matures to black.

© Judy Fulton

© Judy Fulton

Method of spread. Distant spread is by birds and mammals that eat the fruits and expel the seeds in new locations. Local spread is by seed and by new plants emerging from stems that touch the ground and form adventitious roots (layering).

Look-alikes. Native southern arrowwood (*Viburnum dentatum*), smooth arrowwood (*Viburnum dentatum* var. *lucidum*—previously *Viburnum recognitum*), downy arrowwood (*Viburnum rafinesqueanum*), and other opposite-leaved shrubs.

Prevention & Control—Do not purchase or plant these and other invasive viburnums. Hand-pull or dig up seedlings and younger plants, ensuring that the roots are completely removed. Large plants can be extracted using a weed wrench or similar tool. If needed, plants can be cut down and treated with a systemic herbicide applied to freshly cut stems, to kill the entire plant, including the roots.

Native Alternatives—Southern arrowwood (*V. dentatum*), mapleleaf viburnum (*V. acerifolium*), blackhaw (*V. prunifolium*), American elderberry (*Sambucus canadensis*), and witch hazel (*Hamamelis virginiana*). Be aware that viburnum names are often mistaken or interchanged by plant sellers.

TREES

NORWAY MAPLE

Acer platanoides L. / Soapberry family (Sapindaceae)

Amanda Wray

© *Judy Fulton*

Origin—Europe, Western Asia

Background—Norway maple was introduced to the U.S. from England in 1756 by John Bartram for its hardiness, deep shade and adaptability to adverse conditions. It was widely planted on farms and in towns.

Distribution & Habitat—Norway maple has been reported as invasive in natural areas from Minnesota to Maine, south to Tennessee and South Carolina, and in five northwestern states. It has escaped from town plantings into forests, roadsides, and fencerows, and has become a significant component of some eastern forests.

Ecological Threat—Norway maple forms dense, shady monotypic stands that displace native plants and prevent regeneration of native seedlings.

DESCRIPTION & BIOLOGY

Plant. Deciduous tree up to 90' high with a rounded crown and bark that is brown to gray, with a diamond-like pattern.

Leaves. Opposite, palmate (shaped like a hand), *broader across than from tip to base*, 5–7 lobed with attenuated tips and large marginal teeth. *Milky white sap* oozes from cut veins or petioles.

Flowers, fruits & seeds. Flowers are bright yellow-green, about ¼" across, in erect rounded clusters that emerge from stem tips April-May. Fruit is a paired winged samara joined at a wide, nearly 180° angle that matures late summer.

Method of spread. Distant spread is by wind-dispersed seed. Local spread is by seed and vegetative reproduction.

Look-alikes. Native sugar maple (*Acer saccharum*) and red maple (*Acer rubrum*). Norway can be distinguished from other maples by its milky white sap, wide leaves, broadly joined samaras and yellow fall foliage.

Prevention & Control—Do not purchase or plant Norway maple. Pull seedlings and saplings by hand. Cut small to large trees to the ground, repeating as necessary to control any resprouting, or treat cut stems with a systemic herbicide.

Native Alternatives—Red maple (*Acer rubrum*) and sugar maple (*Acer saccharum*).

TREE-OF-HEAVEN
Ailanthus altissimus (Mill.) Swingle / Quassia family (Simaroubaceae)

© Judy Fulton

© Judy Fulton

Origin—Northeastern and central China, Taiwan

Background—Tree-of-heaven, also called ailanthus, shumac, stinking sumac, and Chinese sumac, was introduced in 1748 by a Pennsylvania gardener and was made available commercially by 1840.

Distribution & Habitat—Tree-of-heaven has been reported as invasive in natural areas in the U.S. from coast to coast, in all states except for North and South Dakota, Montana, and Wyoming. It is highly adapted to disturbance, grows best in full sun, can tolerate a wide range of soil types and conditions, is drought-tolerant, and can even grow in a crack on a rock face.

© Judy Fulton   © Judy Fulton

Ecological Threat—Tree-of-heaven grows vigorously, produces abundant seed, and establishes dense clonal or fraternal stands, pushing out native plants. It produces the chemical ailanthone, which has strong allelopathic (herbicidal) effects that impede the growth of other plants nearby. Tree-of-heaven is the preferred host for the Spotted Lanternfly (*Lycorma delicatula*), a highly invasive insect native to China and discovered in the U.S. in 2014.

DESCRIPTION & BIOLOGY

Plant. Deciduous *dioecious* (plant is either male or female) tree to 70' high with smooth, pale gray bark that becomes fissured as it matures. Twigs are stout, light chestnut-brown with dots (lenticels), smooth to slightly pubescent, and have *heart- or shield-shaped leaf scars*. The wood is soft, weak, coarse-grained and creamy white to light brown. Plant parts, including leaves, stems and some flowers, have a *strong, unpleasant odor* likened to rotting peanuts or cashews.

Leaves. Alternate, large (1–4' long), compound, with 11–25 leaflets, each leaflet with one to several glandular teeth near the base.

Flowers, fruits & seeds. Small pale five-petaled flowers with **pistils (female)** or **stamens (male)**, in large branched inflorescences on 20" long stalks; June-July. In summer, clusters of *tan to pinkish-red, single-seeded*, flat but *twisted winged samaras* are produced on female trees and may remain for several months. A mature tree can produce hundreds of thousands of seeds per year.

Method of spread. Distant spread is by seed carried by wind and rainwater. Local spread is by seed and by vigorous resprouting from an extensive root system, especially in response to injury such as breakage or cutting.

Look-alikes. Native shrubs and trees with compound, toothed leaves including staghorn sumac (*Rhus typhina*) with alternate, fuzzy reddish-brown stems and leaves; black walnut (*Juglans nigra*) and hickories (*Carya*) with alternate leaves; and ashes (*Fraxinus*) with opposite leaves.

Prevention & Control—Do not plant tree-of-heaven or spread its seeds when moving soil from infested areas. Before attempting control, *ensure that you are not mistaking native species like sumac, ash, or walnut for tree-of-heaven*. Eliminating ailanthus requires diligence. Pull seedlings and saplings by hand. Target large female trees for control to help reduce spread by seed. Avoid cutting ailanthus because the tree will respond with vigorous resprouting. For trees larger than 2" in diameter, the hack-and-squirt method can be used effectively in summer or fall. A native soil-borne vascular wilt fungus (*Verticillium nonalfalfae*) and an Asian weevil (*Eucryptorrhyncus brandti*) are being studied for potential biological control. The ailanthus webworm (*Atteva aurea*), which is native from Central America to Florida, now occurs in our area, but its effectiveness in controlling ailanthus is not well understood.

Native Alternatives—Shrubs and trees with compound leaves such as sumacs (*Rhus*), hickories (*Carya*), and black walnut (*Juglans nigra*).

SILKTREE

Albizia julibrissin Durazz. / Pea family (Fabaceae)

Origin—Asia

Background—Silktree, also called silky acacia or mimosa, was introduced to the U.S. in 1745 as an ornamental.

Distribution & Habitat—Silktree is reported as invasive in natural areas from Nebraska to Texas and Massachusetts to Florida, and in 6 western states. It grows along forest edges, roadsides and other open habitats and tolerates a variety of soil and moisture conditions.

Ecological Threat—Silktree grows vigorously and displaces native trees and shrubs.

© Bill Johnson

DESCRIPTION & BIOLOGY

Plant. Deciduous, 10–50' high, often multi-trunked tree; bark smooth, thin, and covered with lenticels.

Leaves. Alternate, twice-pinnately compound with sensitive fern-like leaflets that fold at the midrib at night or when touched.

Flowers, fruits & seeds. Small flowers with long pink stamens grouped in tight "pompom-like" clusters; June-July. The fruit is an elongate flat pod up to 6" long with up to a dozen evenly spaced seeds; mature August-September. Seeds are about ¼" long, oval, tan to brown, and long-lived.

Method of spread. Distant spread is by seed. Local spread is by seed and vegetative reproduction.

Look-alikes. Other pea family species including indigo bush (*Amorpha fruticosa*), black locust (*Robinia pseudoacacia*), and forbs like northern wild senna (*Senna hebecarpa*) and sensitive partridge pea (*Chamaecrista nictitans*).

Prevention & Control—Do not purchase or plant silktree. Once established, silktree is difficult to eradicate due to its ability to resprout vigorously. Seedlings can be pulled by hand. Trees can be cut and treated with a systemic herbicide to kill the entire plant including the roots.

Native Alternatives—Downy serviceberry (*Amelanchier arborea*), river birch (*Betula nigra*), redbud (*Cercis canadensis*), fringetree (*Chionanthus virginicus*) and flowering dogwood (*Cornus florida*).

PAPER MULBERRY

Broussonetia papyrifera (L.) Vent. / Mulberry family (Moraceae)

Origin—Japan, Taiwan

Robert Vidéki, bugwood.org

Amy Richard, bugwood.org

Background—Paper mulberry was introduced as a fast-growing ornamental and shade tree. Native Pacific cultures use it to make bark cloth.

Distribution & Habitat—Paper mulberry has been reported as invasive in natural areas from Kansas to Texas and Massachusetts to Florida. It invades forest edges, fields, roadsides, and other disturbed areas, and prefers full sun.

Ecological Threat—Paper mulberry forms dense stands that displace native plants. Its shallow root system makes the tree susceptible to toppling, which can lead to erosion and further invasion.

DESCRIPTION & BIOLOGY

Plant. Deciduous *dioecious* (plant is either male or female) tree to 45–50' tall with tan, smooth, moderately furrowed bark, reddish-brown twigs, soft and brittle wood, and milky sap.

Leaves. Alternate, opposite, or whorled, densely hairy, unlobed to deeply lobed with sharply toothed margins and rounded or heart-shaped leaf bases. The upper surface feels somewhat rough.

Flowers, fruits & seeds. Male and female flowers are produced on separate plants in spring. Male flowers are pale green, fuzzy and in elongate *pendulous catkins*, 2½–3" long. Female flowers are in green *spherical heads* about ¾" across, with long protruding styles. The fruiting structure is a spherical cluster ¾–1" across containing many red or orange protruding fruits (drupes) that mature in summer.

Method of spread. Distant spread is by seed. Local spread is by seed and vegetative sprouting.

Look-alikes. Invasive white mulberry (*Morus alba*); native red mulberry (*Morus rubra*), American basswood (*Tilia americana*) and sassafras (*Sassafras albidum*).

Prevention & Control—Do not plant paper mulberry. Seedlings can be pulled by hand. To prevent resprouting, trees can be cut and treated with a systemic herbicide to kill the entire plant including the roots.

Native Alternatives—Basswood (*Tilia heterophylla*) and sassafras (*Sassafras albidum*).

WHITE MULBERRY

Morus alba L. / Mulberry family (Moraceae)

© Judy Fulton

Jil Swearingen

Origin—China

Background—White mulberry was introduced to the U.S. in the 1600s to establish a silkworm industry, which was unsuccessful. The tree was widely planted throughout the eastern U.S., but in the 1830s cold winters and disease decimated mulberry plantations and put an end to the planting program. However, white mulberry survived outside of cultivation and continued to establish and spread in the wild.

Distribution & Habitat—White mulberry has been reported as invasive in natural areas in all states in the conterminous U.S. except for Nevada. According to the U.S. Forest Service, white mulberry occurs most frequently in mixed-hardwood forest communities, including floodplain, lowland, upland, and ravine forests; forests with eastern white pine and eastern hemlock; and on sand flats. White mulberry has been reported as common or frequent in black locust and oak-maple plant associations, and in floodplain forests dominated by ashes, elms, hackberry, red maple, shingle oak, boxelder, and American sycamore.

© Judy Fulton

TREES

117

Ecological Threat—White mulberry is a large tree and a common component of eastern forests and human-dominated landscapes. While not typically found in dense patches, it displaces native woody and herbaceous plants. More significantly, white mulberry readily hybridizes with red mulberry (*Morus rubra*), which is native throughout the eastern and central U.S.; white mulberry and the hybrid are replacing and outcompeting red mulberry.

DESCRIPTION & BIOLOGY

Plant. Deciduous tree, *dioecious* (plant is either male or female) or sometimes *monoecious* (plant has both male and female flowers), up to 50' tall with thin shallowly furrowed bark and glabrous to pubescent stems. Young bark, inner bark, and bark along the roots is bright orange. Twigs and leaves ooze a milky sap when broken.

Leaves. Alternate, simple, ovate with a heart-shaped base and coarsely serrate margins, unlobed to deeply lobed; upper surface glossy and smooth; lower surface dull and smooth or with very small hairs along veins.

Flowers, fruits & seeds. Flowers occur in spring and are wind-pollinated; male and female flowers are very small and borne in catkins, either on the same tree or on separate trees. Male catkins are about 1–1½" long; female catkins are about ½–¾" long. The fruit, an aggregation of single-seeded drupes, is ½–1" long and can be white, pink, or black and may remain on the tree for several days. The seed is an ovoid nutlet with a thin, soft shell and a hard "bony" coat.

Method of spread. Distant spread is by birds, red foxes, raccoons, Virginia opossums, squirrels, other mammals, and possibly turtles, that eat the fruits and expel the seeds elsewhere. Local spread is by new plants that sprout from stumps, roots and cut stems buried in the soil.

Look-alikes. Native red mulberry (*Morus rubra*), basswood (*Tilia americana*), and sassafras (*Sassafras albidum*); non-native invasive paper mulberry (*Broussonetia papyrifera*).

Prevention & Control—Do not plant white mulberry. Seedlings can be pulled by hand. To prevent resprouting, trees can be cut and treated with a systemic herbicide to kill the entire plant including the roots.

Native Alternatives—Red maple (*Acer rubrum*), hackberry (*Celtis occidentalis*), black gum (*Nyssa sylvatica*) and sassafras (*Sassafras albidum*).

PRINCESS TREE

Paulownia tomentosa (Thunb.) Steud. / Paulownia family (Paulowniaceae)

© Bill Johnson

Leslie Mehrhoff, bugwood.org

Origin—Central and Western China

Background—Princess tree, also known as empress tree and royal paulownia, was imported to Europe by the Dutch East India Company in the 1830s and to North America soon after. Historical records describe important medicinal, ornamental and timber uses of princess tree as early as the third century B.C. For many years, it was planted as an ornamental in the U.S., but in the 1970s it began to be grown as a valuable export product. The wood is easy to work and highly prized for carving.

Distribution & Habitat—Princess tree has been reported as invasive in natural areas from Wisconsin to Texas and Vermont to Florida, and in Washington. It grows in disturbed forests and forest edges, on steep rocky slopes, streambanks, and roadsides. It tolerates infertile, acidic soils and drought.

Ecological Threat—Princess tree displaces native herbaceous and woody plants. It can sprout prolifically from adventitious buds on stems and roots, enabling it to survive fire, cutting, and even bulldozing in construction areas.

DESCRIPTION & BIOLOGY

Plant. Deciduous tree to 60' tall with rough gray-brown bark and stout green to brown or dark gray twigs speckled with white dots (lenticels).

Leaves. Opposite, large, broadly oval to heart-shaped, sometimes shallowly three-lobed; with soft velvety hairs on both surfaces.

© Judy Fulton

Robert Vidéki, bugwood.org

Flowers, fruits & seeds. Flowers are pale violet, 2" long, bilaterally symmetrical with tubular corollas of five fused petals. Inflorescences appear in upright pyramidal clusters 8–12" tall before leaves emerge; April-May. Flowers are fragrant and insect-pollinated. Fruit is an oval 4-compartmented capsule 1–2" long by 1½" wide, in drooping clusters. Capsules are green in summer, turn dark brown, and persist through winter. Capsules split in half in late winter, each releasing up to 2,000 tiny winged seeds. A single mature tree can produce up to 2 million seeds a year. Seeds germinate easily, and seedlings grow and mature quickly, producing flowers in as little as 4–5 years, but more typically within 8–10 years.

Method of spread. Distant spread is by seed transported by wind and water. Local spread is by seed and by root sprouts from adventitious buds on stems and roots.

Look-alikes. Southern catalpa (*Catalpa bignonioides*), native to the southeastern U.S.; Chinese catalpa (*Catalpa ovata*), native to China and invasive in the central and northeastern U.S.

Prevention & Control—Do not purchase or plant princess tree. Seedlings and young plants can be pulled by hand. To prevent resprouting, trees can be cut and treated with a systemic herbicide to kill the entire plant including the roots.

Native Alternatives—American sycamore (*Platanus occidentalis*), umbrella magnolia (*Magnolia tripetala*), and American holly (*Ilex opaca*).

CALLERY PEAR

Pyrus calleryana Dcne. / Rose family (Rosaceae)

© Judy Fulton

© Judy Fulton

Origin—China, Vietnam

Background—Callery pear was first planted in 1909 at the Arnold Arboretum. Large amounts of seed were imported by the U.S. Department of Agriculture 1916-1919 for development of fire blight resistance in the common pear (*Pyrus communis*); the disease was devastating the commercial pear industry. Callery pear was widely planted as a rootstock for common pear long before gaining attention as an ornamental. In 1952, the ornamental value and the hardiness of Callery pear were recognized, leading to commercialization of a number of cultivars starting in the 1960s. Although it is now known that *Pyrus calleryana* is structurally unsound and has a tendency to drop branches, its cultivars are still widely sold as ornamentals.

Cultivars of Callery pear were developed or selected in the U.S. from genotypes imported from China: Bradford pear (*Pyrus calleryana* 'Bradford') is one genotype. While some genotypes are self-incompatible (i.e., they require cross-pollination from another genotype to set seed), others can pollinate themselves. Different genotypes growing near each other (e.g., within about 300') can cross-pollinate and produce fruit with viable seed. Varieties are often grafted onto seed-grown rootstocks from different genotypes. If shoots grow from the rootstock, as often happens, the flowers on these shoots and the graft can pollinate each other. The 'Bradford' pear is one of several Callery pear cultivars capable of spreading and becoming invasive. Because it is propagated asexually by grafting and cuttings, 'Bradford' pear does not evolve over time. Any plant resulting from a seed produced by *Pyrus calleryana* 'Bradford' is a different genotype of *Pyrus calleryana* and not any particular variety, unless someone propagates that seedling and

TREES

© Judy Fulton

names it as a new cultivar. *The plants that spread in natural areas are not cultivars, but sexually reproducing populations consisting of multiple genotypes that recombine every generation.*

Distribution & Habitat—Callery pear has been reported as invasive in natural areas from Wisconsin to Texas and New Hampshire to Florida, and in California, Colorado, Idaho and Utah. It grows best in full sun, but will tolerate some shading and drought.

Ecological Threat—Callery pear is a highly successful invader and forms colonial thickets that push out and exclude native plants; a single tree can spread rapidly, forming a sizable patch within just a few years. Copious amounts of fruits are produced and the seeds are dispersed by birds and possibly small mammals. Seedlings germinate easily and grow rapidly in disturbed areas. Callery pear is relatively free of insect pests and pathogens, except for fire blight.

DESCRIPTION & BIOLOGY

Plant. Deciduous tree with a rounded crown, to 50' tall and 30' wide when mature. Twigs can be smooth or hairy. Thorns, if present, can be up to 3" long, sharp, and strong enough to incapacitate bulldozers by piercing tires.

Leaves. Alternate, simple, 1½–3" long, petiolate, shiny with wavy, slightly toothed margins and a cordate base. Leaves turn scarlet, mahogany, and purple in fall.

Flowers, fruits & seeds. Flowers are 1" wide with five white petals, produced in showy clusters in spring before leaf emergence, and have an unpleasant, sweet-musky odor. Fruit is a small, round, hard, brown pome covered with tiny flecks; matures in fall.

Method of spread. Distant spread is by seeds eaten by starlings and other birds and deposited in new locations. Local spread is by seed and by new shoots produced from the plant's shallow root system.

Look-alikes. Native basswood (*Tilia americana*); non-native cultivated apple (*Malus pumila*); non-native and native crabapples (*Malus*); two non-native pears that are starting to establish and spread in the mid-Atlantic, sometimes in dense stands: **Asian pear (*Pyrus pyrifolia*)** with leaves that are very similar to those of Callery pear, and **birchleaf pear (*Pyrus betulifolia*)** with leaves that are elliptical, toothed, and somewhat narrower than those of Callery pear.

Prevention & Control—Do not purchase or plant Callery pear or any cultivars, including the well-known 'Bradford' pear. Seedlings and saplings can be pulled by hand. Medium to large trees will need to be treated with a systemic herbicide. When working with thorny plants, be sure to wear goggles and tough clothing.

Native Alternatives—Downy serviceberry (*Amelanchier arborea*), Allegheny serviceberry (*Amelanchier laevis*), cockspur hawthorn (*Crataegus crus-galli*), green hawthorn (*C. viridis*), and sweet crabapple (*Malus coronaria*).

SAWTOOTH OAK

Quercus acutissima Carruth. / Beech family (Fagaceae)

© Judy Fulton

© Judy Fulton

Origin—Temperate and tropical Asia

Background—Sawtooth oak was introduced to the U.S. in 1862 as an ornamental. It became recognized for its rapid growth and abundant production of acorns that were thought to be effective in attracting wildlife for hunting. Some hunters and natural resource agencies still promote the species because it bears acorns at a much younger age than native oaks. However, people eventually realized that sawtooth acorns are very bitter and not preferred by most native wildlife. The nutritional value of the acorns is also very low compared to native oaks.

Distribution & Habitat—Sawtooth oak has been reported as invasive in natural areas throughout the eastern U.S. from Michigan to Louisiana and Connecticut to Georgia. It is found in forest edges, forest interiors, and along road-sides, and it readily invades recently cleared areas and other openings. It does best in well drained, sandy-loam and clay-loam soils, and is drought-tolerant. Seedlings will not survive saturation for more than a day.

Ecological Threat—Sawtooth oak is spreading from intentional wildlife plantings and landscapes, and is becoming established in forest edges, forest interiors, fields, meadows, clearings and other habitats. It displaces and excludes native plants and has little nutritional benefit for native animals.

DESCRIPTION & BIOLOGY

Plant. Large, deciduous tree to 60' tall. Stems are smooth; bark is ash brown and becomes ridged and furrowed when mature.

Leaves. Alternate, lance-shaped, 3–7" long by about 2½" wide, with 12-18 pinnate veins that end in bristle-like teeth at the leaf margin. Leaves have a glossy or lacquered appearance, are green during spring and summer, turn yellow in fall, and remain brown through winter.

Flowers, fruits & seeds. Flowers bloom in May; male flowers are in drooping pale yellow catkins; female flowers are small, borne on short spikes, and appear with the leaves. The fruit is an acorn about ¾" across, enclosed by an involucre (cap) with long, coarse, spreading, recurved scales; the cap obscures about ⅔ of the acorn.

Method of spread. Distant spread is by acorns carried away and buried for later consumption by squirrels, (possibly) blue jays, and other animals. Local spread is by acorns dropping from trees that are buried by animals.

Look-alikes. Non-native and invasive Chinese chestnut (*Castanea mollissima*) and zelkova (*Zelkova serrata*); native American chestnut (*Castanea dentata*), Allegheny chinkapin (*Castanea pumila*) and American beech (*Fagus grandifolia*).

Prevention & Control—Do not purchase or plant sawtooth oak. Seedlings can be pulled by hand. To kill the entire plant including the roots, trees can be cut and treated with systemic herbicide.

Native Alternatives—Chestnut oak (*Quercus montana*), white oak (*Quercus alba*), willow oak (*Q. phellos*), and other oak species; shagbark hickory (*Carya ovata*), pignut hickory (*C. glabra*), American beech (*Fagus grandifolia*).

VINES

CHOCOLATE VINE

Akebia quinata (Thunb. ex Houtt.) Decne. / Lardizabala family (Lardizabalaceae)

© Judy Fulton

Origin—Central China, Japan, Korea

Background—Chocolate vine, also known as five-leaf akebia, was imported around 1845 as an ornamental.

Distribution & Habitat—Chocolate vine has been reported as invasive in natural areas from Wisconsin to Louisiana and New Hampshire to Mississippi. It invades forests and is very shade tolerant.

Ecological Threat—Chocolate vine grows along the ground and climbs by twining, forming impenetrable tangles that smother native plants.

DESCRIPTION & BIOLOGY

Plant. Woody, deciduous, perennial, *monoecious* trailing or twining vine, with slender stems that are green when young, becoming brown when mature.

Leaves. Alternate, palmate (like a hand), with five stalked leaflets that meet at a central point on a long leaf stalk; leaflets entire, oval with notched tips, dull blue-green.

Flowers, fruits & seeds. Male and female flowers are separate, pale purple to reddish, ½–1" wide, with chocolate fragrance in spring. Fruit is a soft sausage-like pod, to 4" long in summer.

Method of spread. Distant and local spread is primarily by vegetative means.

Look-alikes. Native Virginia creeper (*Parthenocissus quinquefolia*) and non-native invasive bushkiller (*Cayratia japonica*), both with toothed leaflets.

Prevention & Control—Do not purchase chocolate vine. Hand-pull or dig up vines along with the roots. Treat large infestations with a systemic herbicide.

Native Alternatives—Pipevine (*Aristolochia macrophylla*), trumpet creeper (*Campsis radicans*), coral honeysuckle (*Lonicera sempervirens*).

PORCELAIN-BERRY

Ampelopsis glandulosa (Wall.) Momiy. var. *brevipedunculata* (Maxim.) Momiy. / Grape family (Vitaceae)

© Judy Fulton

© Judy Fulton

Origin—China, Korea, Japan, Russian Far East

Background—Porcelain-berry (synonym *Ampelopsis brevipedunculata*) is also known as Amur peppervine. It was originally cultivated as a bedding and landscape plant. Despite its well-known invasiveness, it is still sold by some nurseries, retailers, and online companies in the U.S.

Distribution & Habitat—Porcelain-berry has been reported as invasive in natural areas from Minnesota to Mississippi, and Maine to Georgia. It invades forest edges, pond margins, streambanks, thickets, and various disturbed areas, and grows well in most soils that are not permanently wet. Porcelain-berry prefers full sun or part shade, and is less tolerant of heavily shaded areas, such as mature forest interiors. Seeds germinate readily in both disturbed open areas and forest interiors when a tree falls and opens the canopy.

Ecological Threat—Porcelain-berry is a vigorous invader of open and forested habitats. It forms thick, impenetrable blankets over native herbaceous and woody plants, weakening and killing them by blocking access to sunlight.

DESCRIPTION & BIOLOGY

Plant. Deciduous, woody, perennial vine with a strong root system; climbs with tendrils and closely resembles grape (*Vitis*). Stems have rough, non-peeling bark (dotted with lenticels when young) and white pith that continues across nodes. Young stems are usually pubescent.

Leaves. Alternate, simple, maple-like with a heart-shape base, toothed margins, 3–5 shallow to deeply cut lobes, shiny above with hairs on veins of leaf underside. Green and white variegated leaves occur infrequently.

Flowers, fruits & seeds. Flowers are small, greenish-white, in flat-topped or slightly rounded clusters in June-August. Fruit is a speckled pink, green, aqua, blue, or purple berry containing 2–4 seeds in September-October.

Method of spread. Distant spread is by birds and mammals that eat the fruits and defecate seeds in new locations. Local spread is by seed or root sprouts.

Look-alikes. Native grapes (*Vitis*, except for *V. rotundifolia*) with *smooth, peeling or shredding bark, tan or brown pith interrupted by a diaphragm at nodes*, and *flowers in panicles*; and other vines with maple-like leaves.

Prevention & Control—Do not purchase porcelain-berry. Its vigorous root system makes it difficult to control. Hand-pull seedlings and young plants along with the entire rootstock. Large vines can be cut and treated with a systemic herbicide. Large infestations may require foliar treatment.

Native Alternatives—Summer grape (*Vitis aestivalis*), possum grape (*V. cinerea*), fox grape (*V. labrusca*).

Young porcelain-berry bark

Mature porcelain-berry bark

Young grape bark

Mature grape bark

Photos by Jil Swearingen

VINES

ASIAN BITTERSWEET

Celastrus orbiculatus Thunb. / Staff-tree family (Celastraceae)

© Bill Johnson

© Judy Fulton

Origin—Eastern Asia, Korea, China, Japan

Background—Asian bittersweet, also known as Oriental bittersweet, round-leaved bittersweet and climbing spindleberry, was introduced to the U.S. in the 1860s as an ornamental and for erosion control. Gardeners and horticulturists planted it widely for making decorative fall wreaths and other items. Despite its well-known invasiveness, it is still available from some local and mail-order nurseries in the U.S. Prior to Asian bittersweet's arrival, American bittersweet (*Celastrus scandens*) was the only native vine member of the staff-tree family in the U.S. and occurred throughout the central and eastern states. American and Asian bittersweet have been confirmed to hybridize under laboratory conditions. Genetic field studies are needed to confirm hybridization in the wild.

Distribution & Habitat—Asian bittersweet has been reported as invasive in natural areas from Minnesota to Louisiana, and Maine to Georgia. It is found in mesic, mixed hardwood forests and forest edges, coniferous forests, disturbed woods, old fields, dunelands, coastal beaches, and tidal freshwater and saltmarsh communities. Asian bittersweet grows under a wide range of light conditions. Laboratory studies have determined that its seeds can germinate under very low to full sunlight levels, which would allow the plant to survive in forest interiors under closed canopy conditions.

Ecological Threat—Asian bittersweet grows vigorously, forming heavy tangles over vegetation and creating dense shade that weakens and kills plants. It can kill trees and shrubs by girdling, and the excess weight of the vines can lead to uprooting and toppling. Other effects include raising soil pH (making the soil more basic), increasing nitrogen mineralization, accelerating litter decomposition, and altering nesting habitat for native birds. Asian bittersweet has replaced American bittersweet throughout much of the native's historic range as a result of competition, hybridization or both.

DESCRIPTION & BIOLOGY

Plant. Deciduous, *dioecious* (plant is either male or female), woody vine that climbs by twining around stems and trunks without tendrils or other attachment structures. It can grow to 66', and older plants can become very large, with stem diameters up to 4". It also grows as a shrub on sand dunes and beaches. Roots are orange, except on new seedlings.

Leaves. Alternate, glossy and rounded with finely toothed margins.

Flowers, fruits & seeds. Small, greenish flowers in clusters emerge from most leaf axils; May-June. Male and female flowers are on separate plants. The fruit is a globular, dehiscent, 3-valved capsule that matures, turns yellow in late summer-early fall, and splits open to reveal a fleshy, red-orange aril covering 1–2 seeds. Fruits can persist on vines through winter, and seeds germinate in late spring.

Method of spread. Distant spread is by birds that eat the fruits and expel the seeds elsewhere, and by people who improperly dispose of wreaths and other decorations made with Asian bittersweet. Local spread is through dropped seeds and sprouting from roots, root fragments, and the root crown.

Look-alikes. American bittersweet (*Celastrus scandens*), which produces flowers and fruits only at the tips of stems.

Prevention & Control—Do not buy or plant Asian bittersweet. If you purchase a wreath or other decorative item laden with bittersweet fruits, bag and dispose of it in the trash rather than outdoors. Pull seedlings and young plants up by hand. Older vines can be removed using a shovel, pitch fork, mattock, weed wrench, or other tool to help loosen the roots or cut and treated with a systemic herbicide.

Native Alternatives—Although American bittersweet (*Celastrus scandens*) would otherwise be an excellent alternative, most botanists and ecologists recommend against planting it where Asian bittersweet occurs, due to the risk of hybridization. Nurseries may mislabel Asian bittersweet as the native species.

Jil Swearingen

SWEET AUTUMN CLEMATIS

Clematis terniflora DC / Buttercup family (Ranunculaceae)

© Judy Fulton

© Judy Fulton

Origin—Japan, China

Background—Sweet autumn clematis, also known as sweet autumn or yam-leaved virgin's bower, was introduced into the U.S. in the late 1800s as an ornamental vine. It is still sold in the nursery trade. Four other introduced species of clematis have been reported to be invasive in the U.S.: *C. flammula*, *C. orientalis*, *C. tangutica*, and *C. vitalba*.

Distribution & Habitat—Sweet autumn clematis has been reported invasive in natural areas from Minnesota to Texas, and Maine to Florida. It invades forest edges, streambanks, riparian areas, and rights-of-way, and grows best in moist soil in full sun.

Ecological Threat—Sweet autumn clematis grows vigorously, climbing over other vegetation and forming thick blanketing tangles from the ground to the tree canopy. Its dense growth kills native plants by blocking sunlight and can lead to toppling from excess weight.

DESCRIPTION & BIOLOGY

Plant. Deciduous to semi-evergreen perennial vine that climbs by twining, without tendrils or other attachment structures.

Leaves. Opposite, usually pinnately compound with 5 entire (non-toothed), ovate to elliptic, somewhat leathery leaflets, each 2–3" long.

Flowers, fruits & seeds. Flowers have four white slender *sepals* (not petals) produced in axillary and terminal panicle; July-September. The fruit is a dry, indehiscent achene adorned with a feathery plume-like structure; matures August-October and persists into winter.

Method of spread. Distant spread is by wind-dispersed achenes. Local spread is by seed or by vegetative growth of stolons.

Look-alikes. Native virgin's bower (*Clematis virginiana*), with trifoliate or pinnate leaves and leaflets with toothed margins, sometimes lobed. Non-native garden clematis with large, showy colorful flowers.

Prevention & Control—Do not purchase or plant sweet autumn clematis. Vines can be pulled by hand or cut near the ground to kill climbing stems. Use caution since sap can cause contact dermatitis. An herbicide might be needed for large infestations.

Native Alternatives—Virgin's bower (*Clematis virginiana*).

WINTERCREEPER

Euonymus fortunei (Turkz.) Hand.-Mazz. / Bittersweet family (Celastraceae)

© Judy Fulton

© Judy Fulton

Origin—China, Japan, Korea

Background—Wintercreeper, also known as creeping euonymus, was introduced to the U.S. in 1907 as an ornamental. It grows as a creeping, sprawling vine or shrub. Wintercreeper can climb high into trees, attaching to bark with aerial adventitious rootlets. Wintercreeper has escaped from gardens and landscapes into natural areas and is a highly invasive species.

Distribution & Habitat—Wintercreeper has been reported as invasive in natural areas from Minnesota to Nebraska and Texas, and Maine to Florida. It grows in forest habitats in full sun to deep shade, prefers well-drained soil, and is tolerant of acidic to basic and low-nutrient soils.

Amanda Wray © *Judy Fulton*

Ecological Threat—Wintercreeper invades upland and lowland forests. It can remain a small plant until an event opens up the canopy, increasing sunlight and stimulating it to grow. As a groundcover, it forms a monoculture that displaces and excludes native plants. As a climbing vine it grows on trunks and branches and can lead to weakening and toppling of trees. Forest openings are especially vulnerable to invasion.

DESCRIPTION & BIOLOGY

Plant. Evergreen, woody vine or sprawling shrub, with green stems that become light gray and corky with age. It climbs trees using aerial adventitious roots produced at stem nodes.

Leaves. Opposite, oval, about 1–2½" long, glossy, dark green with lighter veins and slightly toothed margins.

Flowers, fruits & seeds. Flowers bloom May-July and are about ¼" across, each with four pale green petals, four green sepals, four spreading stamens, and a single green, square-shaped pistil; May-July. Fruits are small, round, white to pinkish-red capsules that split open to expose seeds with reddish-orange arils; late summer into fall, typically on climbing plants.

Method of spread. Distant spread is by birds and other wildlife that eat the fruits and defecate the seeds in new locations, and by seeds transported by water. Local spread is through formation of new plants from rootlets on stems touching the ground.

Look-alikes. Native strawberry bush (*Euonymus americanus*) and eastern wahoo (*Euonymus atropurpureus*); non-native invasive winged burning bush

(*Euonymus alatus*), common periwinkle (*Vinca minor*), largeleaf periwinkle (*Vinca major*), and Japanese honeysuckle (*Lonicera japonica*).

Prevention & Control—Do not purchase or plant winter creeper. Plants can be pulled by hand, dug up, or mowed. Vines on trees should be cut near the ground to kill climbing portions. If needed, stems can be cut and treated with a systemic herbicide to kill the entire plant including the roots.

Native Alternatives—Trumpet creeper (*Campsis radicans*).

ENGLISH IVY

Hedera helix L. / Ginseng family (Araliaceae)

© Judy Fulton © Judy Fulton

Origin—Europe, Western Asia, Northern Africa

Background—European colonists introduced English ivy as early as 1727. It is widely planted for its evergreen foliage and dependability as a year-round low-maintenance groundcover. Although it is recognized as a serious invader of natural ecosystems, parks, and landscapes, English ivy continues to be marketed and sold as an ornamental in the U.S. Two other species of *Hedera* are recognized as invasive in the U.S.: Atlantic ivy (*H. hibernica*), which is difficult to distinguish from English ivy, and Canary Island ivy (*H. canariensis*).

Distribution & Habitat—English ivy has been reported as invasive in natural areas from Minnesota to Texas and Maine to Florida, and in Arizona, California, Colorado, Oregon, Utah and Washington. It flourishes under shady to full sun conditions in moist and moderately fertile soils, but is intolerant of drought and salinity. Invaded habitats include forest openings and edges, fields, cliffs, steep slopes, and various disturbed areas. Due to similar appearances, Atlantic ivy may sometimes have been reported as English ivy.

© Judy Fulton

Ecological Threat—English ivy is a vigorously growing vine that threatens all vegetation levels of forested and open areas, from the ground to the canopy. As a groundcover, it forms a monoculture of ropey vines rooted to the soil, pushing out and excluding almost all other vegetation. Vines climbing on trees spread out and envelop branches and twigs. By blocking sunlight from reaching the host tree's foliage, the vines weaken and eventually kill the infested tree. An infested tree may exhibit decline for several to many years before dying. The added weight of vines also makes trees susceptible to toppling and uprooting during storms. English ivy has been confirmed as a reservoir for bacterial leaf scorch (*Xylella fastidiosa*), a harmful plant pathogen that affects a wide variety of native and ornamental trees such as elms, oaks and maples.

DESCRIPTION & BIOLOGY

Plant. Evergreen, perennial, climbing and sprawling vine that attaches to bark, brickwork, siding and other surfaces by root-like structures that exude a glue-like substance. The leaves and berries of English ivy contain the glycoside hederin, which may cause toxicosis if ingested. Symptoms include gastrointestinal upset, diarrhea, hyperactivity, breathing difficulty, coma, fever, polydipsia, dilated pupils, muscular weakness, and lack of coordination. This chemical may facilitate defecation of the seeds by birds.

Leaves. Alternate, dark green with whitish veins, waxy, somewhat leathery. Leaves growing along the ground are typically 3–5 lobed; leaves of climbing vines are unlobed or slightly lobed.

Flowers, fruits & seeds. Flowers small, greenish-yellow, grouped in globular, starburst-like inflorescences at stem tips; late summer-early fall, typically under sunny conditions. European honeybees and other insects are attracted to the flowers. Fruit is a blue-black berry with a fleshy outer layer and stone-like seeds.

Method of spread. Distant spread is by birds that consume the fruits and expel them in new locations. Local spread is by seed and vegetative growth at stem tips.

Look-alikes. Native poison ivy (*Toxicodendron radicans*) with deciduous "leaflets of three" and hairy stems; non-native invasive Atlantic ivy (*Hedera hibernica*) and Boston ivy (*Parthenocissus japonicus*).

Prevention & Control—Do not buy or plant English ivy. Plants can be pulled by hand, raked up or mowed. Gloves should be worn to protect from sap that may cause contact dermatitis and from poison ivy that often grows with it. Pulled vines can be piled up and allowed to desiccate and rot. Vines growing up tree trunks can be cut low to kill climbing portions. Cut surfaces can be treated with systemic herbicide to kill the roots.

Jil Swearingen

Native Alternatives—Virginia creeper (*Parthenocissus quinquefolia*), Virginia strawberry (*Fragaria virginiana*), American alumroot (*Heuchera americana*), golden ragwort (*Packera aurea*).

JAPANESE HOP

Humulus japonicus Siebold & Zucc. / Hemp family (Cannabaceae)

Leslie Mehrhoff, bugwood.org

© Judy Fulton

VINES

Origin—Temperate and tropical Asia

Background—Japanese hop was originally imported to the U.S. in the late 1800s as an ornamental vine.

Distribution & Habitat—Japanese hop has been reported as invasive in natural areas from Minnesota to Kansas, and Maine to Alabama. It prefers full sun, moist, rich soil, and is commonly found along streambanks and floodplains. Growth is less vigorous in shade and on drier soils.

Ecological Threat—Japanese hop can spread rapidly to cover large areas of open ground and low vegetation, including understory shrubs and small trees. Many thousands of plants can cover a single acre. It grows vigorously during the summer and can form dense mats several feet deep, creating deep shade for plants underneath. Hop vines twining around shrubs and trees can cause them to break or fall over. Japanese hop is invasive in riparian and floodplain habitats, where it displaces native vegetation, prevents the emergence of new plants, and kills newly-planted trees installed for streamside habitat restoration. Hop can also cover small trees and impede mowing and herbicide applications.

DESCRIPTION & BIOLOGY

Plant. Herbaceous, *dioecious* (plant is either male or female), usually annual, shallow-rooted, twining vine with hairy, rough-textured stems covered with short, sharp, downward-pointing prickles. It sprawls over the ground and over low vegetation, and climbs plants and structures to heights of 10' or more. The prickles can be very irritating to the skin.

Leaves. Opposite, simple, rough-textured, palmate (like a hand) with 5–7 lobes, coarsely toothed margins and long leaf stalks.

Flowers, fruits & seeds. Male and female flowers are on separate plants in July-August. Female flowers lack petals and are contained in soft, plump, hairy, drooping cone-like clusters ¾–1½" long, called "hops". Each flower is surrounded by a pale green, tapered, sparsely hairy and gland-dotted leafy bract. Male flowers are tiny (about ⅛" wide) and in upright panicles to 1' long. Each female flower produces a single seed that matures in late summer and persists through winter. Seeds begin to germinate in early spring. If sufficient sunlight and moisture are available, new plants may continue to emerge as the season progresses.

Method of spread. Distant spread is by seed dispersed by animals, machinery and floodwaters to new locations. Local spread is by abundant fruit dropping from vines.

Look-alikes. Native common hop (*Humulus lupulus*) with 3-lobed or unlobed leaves and a shorter leaf stalk; and oneseed bur cucumber (*Sicyos angulatus*) with shallow-lobed leaves and stems with tendrils that lack prickles.

Prevention & Control—Do not plant Japanese hop. Plants can be pulled by hand, wearing gloves to protect skin from prickles. Large patches may need to be treated with a systemic herbicide that kills the entire plant including the roots.

Native Alternatives—Common hop (*Humulus lupulus*), common moonseed (*Menispermum canadense*), yellow passionflower (*Passiflora lutea*).

JAPANESE HONEYSUCKLE

Lonicera japonica Thunb. / Honeysuckle family (Caprifoliaceae)

© Judy Fulton

Jil Swearingen

Origin—China, Japan, Korea

Background—Japanese honeysuckle is a perennial ornamental vine introduced in 1806 to Long Island, New York, and is one of the most widespread and recognizable plants in the U.S.

Distribution & Habitat—Japanese honeysuckle has been reported as invasive in natural areas from Wisconsin to Texas and Maine to Florida, and in Arizona, California, Nevada, New Mexico, Utah and Washington. It is adapted to a wide variety of habitats and grows best in full sun, but can tolerate deep shade.

Ecological Threat—Japanese honeysuckle is a vigorous, fast-growing vine that forms large smothering tangles over native vegetation and twines around woody plants, frequently leading to girdling.

DESCRIPTION & BIOLOGY

Plant. Perennial, deciduous to semi-evergreen twining vine with pubescent, reddish brown to light brown stems.

Leaves. Opposite, ovate to oblong-ovate, about 1–3" long by ½–1½" wide, with entire margins, except for young leaves, which are often deeply lobed.

Flowers, fruits & seeds. Flowers are tubular and bilobed with 4 fused petals above and a single petal below; in pairs in leaf axils; white, turning yellow with age; highly fragrant with copious nectar; spring-summer. Fruits are paired, black, about ¼" in diameter, each with 2–3 flattened oval seeds that ripen in fall.

VINES

Method of spread. Distant spread is by birds that eat the fruits and expel seeds in new locations. Local spread is through fallen fruits, rhizome growth, and runners that develop roots at stem nodes coming in contact with moist soil.

Look-alikes. Native coral honeysuckle (*Lonicera sempervirens*) with terminal clusters of long, showy red tubular flowers.

Prevention & Control—Plants can be pulled by hand, mowed, or treated with systemic herbicide.

Native Alternatives—Coral honeysuckle (*Lonicera sempervirens*), trumpet creeper (*Campsis radicans*), crossvine (*Bignonia capreolata*).

MILE-A-MINUTE

Persicaria perfoliata (L.) H. Gross / Buckwheat family (Polygonaceae)

© Judy Fulton

© Judy Fulton

Origin—Temperate and tropical eastern Asia

Background—Mile-a-minute (synonym *Polygonum perfoliatum* L.) is also known as devil's-tail tearthumb and Asiatic tearthumb. It was introduced to a nursery site in York County, Pennsylvania, in the 1930s. That introduction is thought to be the source of this invasive plant in the mid-Atlantic and northeastern U.S. Seeds are easily spread by birds and may have been spread with rhododendron stock.

Distribution & Habitat—Mile-a-minute has been reported as invasive in natural areas from New Hampshire to North Carolina—with Pennsylvania as the epicenter—and in Ohio, Indiana, Iowa and Oregon. It invades fields, forest edges, streambanks, wetlands, roadsides, and open, disturbed areas.

Ecological Threat—Mile-a-minute grows rapidly, up to 6" a day, and produces a thick smothering tangle of vines over native vegetation, weakening and eventually killing covered plants by blocking sunlight.

DESCRIPTION & BIOLOGY

Plant. Herbaceous, annual, trailing vine with delicate green to pink or reddish stems armed with recurved barbs that are also present on the undersides of leaves. A distinctive circular, leafy structure called an *ocrea* wraps around the stem at nodes.

Leaves. Alternate, triangular, pale green, on long, delicate, barbed petioles.

Flowers, fruits & seeds. Flowers are small, whitish-green, self-fertilizing, and emerge from the ocrea in June-October. Fruit is a blue, violet or red-purple berry, about ¼" wide, arranged in clusters at the ends of stems. Each fruit contains a single black to reddish-black hard seed (achene) with an elaiosome (a nutritious, lipid-rich food body attractive to ants).

Method of spread. Distant spread is by birds, squirrels, chipmunks, deer and possibly other wildlife that eat the fruits and expel seeds in new locations. Local spread is by at least one species of ant that is attracted to the elaiosome and carries the seed to its nest. Fruits can float and may remain buoyant for up to 9 days, allowing for long-distance movement by water.

Look-alikes. Other plants with triangular-shaped leaves, such as native arrowleaf tearthumb (*Persicaria sagittata*).

Prevention & Control—Plants can be easily pulled by hand and balled up, wearing gloves and long sleeves to protect from the recurved barbs. Pulled plants can be left in a pile to desiccate and monitored the following year for new plants sprouting from seed. A *biocontrol agent*, the tiny weevil (*Rhinoncomimus latipes*), has been released throughout the Northeast and Mid-Atlantic with mixed results. The insect can weaken plants resulting in reduced vegetative growth and fruit production. A plant pathogen (*Colletotrichum gloeosporioides*) from Turkey is being studied as a potential biocontrol.

Native Alternatives—Yellow passionflower (*Passiflora lutea*), moonflower (*Menispermum canadense*).

KUDZU

Pueraria montana (Lour.) Merr. var. *lobata* (Willd.) Maesen & S.M. Almeida ex Sanjappa & Predeep / Pea family (Fabaceae)

© Judy Fulton

© Judy Fulton

Origin—Temperate Asia, tropical Asia, southwestern Pacific

Background—Kudzu was introduced from Japan to the U.S. in 1876 at the Philadelphia Centennial Exposition as an ornamental and in the early 1900s as a forage crop plant. In the 1930s and 1940s, the Soil Conservation Service paid southern farmers to plant kudzu to reduce soil erosion on deforested lands, resulting in over 1 million acres being planted. By the 1950s, it had earned the nickname "the vine that ate the South," and was removed from the Agricultural Conservation Program's list of acceptable species. Kudzu was designated a federal noxious weed by the U.S. Congress in 1998.

Distribution & Habitat—Kudzu has been reported as invasive in natural areas from Nebraska to Texas and Massachusetts to Florida, and in Oregon and Washington. Preferred habitats are open, sunny areas like forest edges, abandoned fields, roadsides, and various disturbed areas. Kudzu does best where winters are mild, summer temperatures are above 80°F, and annual rainfall is 40" or more.

Ecological Threat—Kudzu is a vigorous vine with large leaves that grows to the tree canopy, creating a dense shady blanket over native vegetation, depriving covered plants of sunlight, and making trees susceptible to toppling.

DESCRIPTION & BIOLOGY

Plant. Perennial climbing vine that can grow 60–100' in a year. Mature stems can reach 7" in diameter; roots are fleshy with massive tap roots that can grow to 6' long by 7" across, and weigh up to 400 lbs.

Leaves. Alternate, deciduous, compound, with three broad, often lobed leaflets up to 4" across. Leafstalks and leaf margins are hairy; the terminal leaflet has a longer leaf stalk than the basal pair of leaflets.

Flowers, fruits & seeds. Flowers are purple, about ½" long, with a sweet grapey odor, and are borne in long racemes, in July-October. The fruit is a flat hairy pod about 2" long with 3 hard seeds; pods are in clusters of 20–30. Flowers and fruits form only on vertical climbing vines and plants typically begin to flower when 3 or more years of age.

Method of spread. Distant spread is by seed where the *giant resin bee* (*Megachile sculpturalis*), a kudzu pollinator introduced from eastern Asia and discovered in the U.S. in 1994, is present. Local spread is through runners and rhizomes. New plants can also sprout from the crowns of ground-hugging stems.

Look-alikes. Native poison ivy (*Toxicodendron radicans* ssp. *radicans*) with leaflets of three.

© Judy Fulton © Bill Johnson

VINES

Prevention & Control—Do not plant kudzu. For successful long-term control, the extensive root system must be destroyed. Any remaining root crowns can lead to reinfestation. Mechanical methods include frequent mowing and repeated cutting of vines just above ground level. For large infestations, a systemic herbicide that kills the entire plant including the roots may be needed.

Native Alternatives—Moonseed (*Menispermum canadense*), yellow passion-flower (*Passiflora lutea*).

COMMON PERIWINKLE

Vinca minor L. / Dogbane family (Apocynaceae)

© Bill Johnson

Origin—Europe, western Asia

Background—Common periwinkle was first introduced into the U.S. in the 1700s as an ornamental groundcover. Although it escapes from plantings and is known to be invasive, it is still widely available commercially.

Distribution & Habitat—Common periwinkle has been reported as invasive in natural areas from Minnesota to Texas and Maine to Florida, and in several western states. It invades open to shady sites in forests, forest margins, and disturbed areas, and prefers moist organic soils. It tolerates high temperatures and full shade.

Ecological Threat—Periwinkle grows vigorously, forming a dense groundcover that displaces native plants.

DESCRIPTION & BIOLOGY

Plant. Evergreen, perennial, stoloniferous plant that grows along the ground and produces erect stems up to 6" or more high.

Leaves. Opposite, oval to elliptical, glossy, dark green or sometimes variegated green and white, up to 1¾" long and 1" wide.

Flowers, fruits & seeds. Flowers are pinwheel-shaped with 5 blunt-tipped petals, blue or blue-violet, sometimes white, about 1" across in March-April. Fruits and seeds are rarely produced.

Method of spread. Spread is by rhizomes, by arching stolons that root from the tips, and possibly by stolon fragments. It is also spread in yard waste.

Look-alikes. Non-native, invasive largeleaf periwinkle (*Vinca major*), and wintercreeper (*Euonymus fortunei*).

Prevention & Control—Do not purchase or plant common periwinkle. Plants can be pulled by hand or dug up. Be sure to remove all the rhizomes to prevent regrowth. Repeated mowing may be an effective option. Periwinkle is susceptible to an aggressive pathogen that causes vine stem canker blight.

Native Alternatives—Many native plants, depending on site conditions.

VINES

BLACK SWALLOW-WORT

Vincetoxicum nigrum (L.) Moench / Dogbane family (Apocynaceae)

Origin—Mediterranean regions of France, Italy, Spain

Background—Black swallow-wort (synonym *Cynanchum louiseae*) also known as black dog-strangling vine, was introduced as an ornamental in the 1800s. Early U.S. collections include a record from 1864, Essex County, Massachusetts, describing the plant as "escaping from the botanic garden where it is a weed and promising to become naturalized." In 1867, *Gray's Manual of Botany*, 5th edition, reported the vine as "a weed escaping from gardens in the Cambridge, Massachusetts area."

Leslie Mehrhoff, bugwood.org

Distribution & Habitat—Black swallow-wort has been reported as invasive in natural areas from Minnesota to Kansas and Maine to Virginia, and in southern California. Infestations along the Appalachian Trail in Pennsylvania and elsewhere are a concern due to the potential for spread along the entire AT. Black swallow-wort occurs primarily in upland habitats and invades fields, grassy slopes, forests and forest edges, streambanks, and open disturbed areas. Although it typically occurs in areas dominated by limestone bedrock, black swallow-wort is also found on acidic rock substrates and sandy soils. In particular, it grows in habitats subjected to hydrologic extremes, including alvar communities, rocky outcrops and coastal areas. Black swallow-wort grows best in well-drained, stony soils in sunny, open areas but can tolerate some shade.

Ecological Threat—Black swallow-wort forms dense tangled mats over native vegetation, weakening and eventually killing covered plants by blocking sunlight needed for photosynthesis. The plant is *allelopathic*: it releases chemicals that can hinder the growth of surrounding plants. Infestations displace native plants and degrade wildlife habitat, resulting in serious impacts to rare animal species like the monarch butterfly (*Danaus plexippus*). Black swallow-wort is very similar to native milkweeds (*Asclepias*) that are essential larval host plants for the monarch. Casagrande and Dacey (2007) found that female monarchs sometimes laid eggs on black swallow-wort but the larvae did not survive. According to the Monarch Joint Venture, laboratory tests show that monarch caterpillars cannot survive feeding on either pale or black swallow-wort, making these invasives an ecological "sink" for the monarch butterfly. Swallow-wort infestations also degrade and destroy grassland bird habitat.

Documented impacts on rare, threatened, and endangered plants include:

- Outcompeting a Vermont population of Jessup's milkvetch (*Astragalus robbinsii*), an endemic, federally endangered species
- Overgrowing a population of the federally-listed Hart's tongue fern (*Asplenium scolopendrium* var. *scolopendrium*) in Split Rock, New York
- Threatening to displace the only New England population of green milkweed (*Asclepias viridiflora*) in the state of Connecticut, where green milkweed is listed as an endangered plant

DESCRIPTION & BIOLOGY

Plant. Herbaceous perennial twining vine with pubescent stems; stem hairs often in longitudinal bands; and clear watery sap (unlike the milky sap of milkweeds in the genus *Asclepias*).

Leaves. Opposite, simple, 2–5" long by 1–2½" wide, dark green, shiny, oblong or ovate with a rounded or nearly heart-shaped base, tapered tip and short petiole (about ½" long). The largest leaves are in the middle of the stem. Leaves are smooth or have light pubescence on leaf margins and major veins on leaf undersides.

Flowers, fruits & seeds. Flower buds are globose with a rounded apex, and unopened petals are not twisted. Flowers are ***purple to almost black***, star-shaped, about ¼" across, with 5 triangular, downy petals that are about as long as they are wide. Flower stalks are less than 1" long and usually curved and hairy. Fruits are paired, slender, smooth (hairless), tapered pods about 1½" long. Seeds are about ¼" long, dark brown, flattened, with a narrow membranous wing on the margin and a silky filament at the tip.

Method of spread. Distant and local spread is by wind-dispersed seed.

Look-alikes. Native honeyvine (*Cynanchum laeve*), with heart-shaped leaves and white flowers; non-native invasive pale swallow-wort (*Vincetoxicum rossicum*).

Prevention & Control—Do not plant black or other non-native swallow-worts. Plants can be pulled by hand or dug up. For large infestations, a systemic herbicide is often needed to kill the entire plant including the roots. An insect ***biocontrol agent***, the moth (*Hypena opulenta*) has been released in Canada and is under consideration for approval in the U.S. A fungal pathogen (*Colletotrichum lineola*) is being studied as a potential biocontrol.

Native Alternatives—Honeyvine (*Cynanchum laeve*), common milkweed (*Asclepias syriaca*), and other native milkweed species.

PALE SWALLOW-WORT

Vincetoxicum rossicum (Kleopow ex A. W. Hill) Barbar. / Dogbane family (Apocynaceae)

Leslie Mehrhoff, bugwood.org

Leslie Mehrhoff, bugwood.org

Origin—Southeast Ukraine, Russia

Background—Pale swallow-wort (synonym *Cynanchum rossicum*), also known as pale dog-strangling vine, was first collected in the northeastern U.S. from Monroe and Nassau Counties, New York, in 1897.

Distribution & Habitat—Pale swallow-wort has been reported as invasive in natural areas from southern Maine to northern Maryland, and in Illinois and Minnesota. It is associated with upland habitats that have calcareous soils and it invades fields, grassy slopes, forests and forest edges, streambanks, and open disturbed areas. Plants grow in full sun or under forest canopies and can form dense stands in all light conditions. Well-drained, stony soils are frequently densely colonized, but pale swallow-wort can tolerate a broad moisture range.

Ecological Threat—Pale swallow-wort forms dense tangles that smother and kill native plants. The plant is *allelopathic*: it releases chemicals that can hinder the growth of surrounding plants. According to the Monarch Joint Venture, laboratory tests show that monarch caterpillars cannot survive feeding on either pale or black swallow-wort, making these invasives an ecological "sink" for the monarch butterfly. Infestations of pale swallow-wort also reduce biodiversity by degrading and destroying grassland bird and other wildlife habitat, and by outcompeting rare, threatened and endangered plant species.

DESCRIPTION & BIOLOGY

Plant. Herbaceous perennial twining vine with clear watery sap (unlike the milky sap of milkweeds in the genus *Asclepias*).

VINES

Leslie Mehrhoff, bugwood.org

Leslie Mehrhoff, bugwood.org

Leaves. Opposite, simple, entire (non-toothed margins), 2–5" long, dark green, shiny, oval to elliptic with a pointed tip, and 2–8" long leaf stalks. Leaf margins and major veins on leaf undersides are pubescent.

Flowers, fruits & seeds. Flower buds are ovoid to cone-shaped with a pointed tip; unopened petals are twisted. Flowers are pink to reddish-brown, star-shaped, about ¼" across, with 5 triangular petals that are longer than wide. The fruit is a slender, smooth (hairless) pod about 1½–3" long, usually one pair per flower. Pods turn from green to light brown as they mature, then split open along a ventral suture to release seeds. Seeds are light to dark brown, about ⅓" long, flattened or concave on one side and convex on the other, wider towards tip, with a tiny membranous marginal wing and a silky filament at the tip.

Method of spread. Distant spread is by wind-dispersed seed.

Look-alikes. Native honeyvine (*Cynanchum laeve*), with heart-shaped leaves and white flowers; non-native invasive black swallow-wort (*Vincetoxicum nigrum*).

Prevention & Control—Do not plant pale or other exotic swallow-worts. Plants can be pulled by hand or dug up. For large infestations, a systemic herbicide is often needed to kill the entire plant including the roots. An insect **biocontrol agent**, the moth (*Hypena opulenta*) has been released in Canada and is under consideration for approval in the U.S. A fungal pathogen (*Colletotrichum lineola*) is being studied as a potential biocontrol.

Native Alternatives—Honeyvine (*Cynanchum laeve*), common milkweed (*Asclepias syriaca*) and other native milkweeds.

ASIAN WISTERIAS

Japanese Wisteria (*Wisteria floribunda* (Willd.) DC.) / Chinese Wisteria (*Wisteria sinensis* (Sims) DC.) / Hybrid Wisteria (*Wisteria* x *formosa* Rehder) / Pea family (Fabaceae)

Robert Vidéki

Chinese wisteria

Origin—**Japanese**: Japan, Korea; **Chinese**: China

Background—Chinese and Japanese wisteria were introduced to the U.S. in 1816 and 1830, respectively, as ornamental vines. They have been widely cultivated for their attractive pendulous flowers and for their use in arbors. Both species have escaped plantings and are recognized as extremely weedy in landscapes and natural areas. Additionally, Japanese and Chinese wisteria have interbred to produce a hybrid (*W. x formosa*) that is also weedy and invasive. Silky wisteria (*W. brachybotrys*), a Japanese introduction with short racemes of white or violet-colored flowers, has been reported to have invasive tendencies in gardens and could become a problem in natural areas. Despite the known weedy and invasive tendencies of most Asian wisterias, Japanese, Chinese and named-hybrid wisterias are still often sold by nurseries, big box stores and online sellers.

Distribution & Habitat—Japanese, Chinese, and wild hybrid wisterias have been reported as invasive in natural areas in a combined area generally encompassing Michigan to Texas and Maine to Florida. However, because identifying them is difficult and they are often confused, reported distributions are probably inaccurate. Further, Alan Weakley (2020) noted that wisteria hybrids are common in North America and may occur more frequently than either parent species. Wisterias prefer full sun, but established vines will persist and reproduce in partial shade. They grow best in deep, loamy, well-drained soils, but tolerate a

VINES

Chinese wisteria ascends to the right

Japanese wisteria ascends to the left

variety of soil and moisture conditions. Wisterias infest forest edges, roadsides, rights-of-way and other habitats, especially near arboreta, gardens, commercial and residential developments, and other human-affected landscapes.

Ecological Threat—Wisteria grows vigorously, scrambling over low vegetation and climbing shrubs, trees and structures by twining. The strong woody stems wind tightly around host tree trunks and branches, pressing on the vascular tissue, causing death by girdling. The excess weight of the vines can also cause toppling. New vines germinating from seed or sprouting from rootstocks form dense thickets that smother and shade out native vegetation and impede the growth of natural plant communities. The death of girdled trees creates gaps in the forest canopy, resulting in increased sunlight reaching the ground. This sudden increase in light stimulates the growth of wisteria and other invasives.

Japanese wisteria

DESCRIPTION & BIOLOGY

Plant. Deciduous, perennial woody vines that scramble along the ground and climb 30–70' high by twining, without tendrils, hairs or other attachment structures. Older stems can grow up to 15" in diameter.

Leaves. Alternate, pinnately-compound with varying numbers of paired leaflets and a single terminal leaflet. Leaflets are ovate (egg-shaped) with wavy margins and strongly tapering tips.

Flowers, fruits & seeds. Pale blue, blue-violet, lavender or white "pea" flowers in pendulous racemes typically 4–24" long. Fruits are flattened, fuzzy light brown pods with fuzzy seeds.

Method of spread. Distant spread is by movement of fruits, seeds and plants by water or people. Local spread is by seed and by vegetative growth from vine stems and stolons that root at nodes, or stems that sprout from stumps or root fragments.

Look-alikes. Native American wisteria (*W. frutescens*) and other plants with pinnately-compound leaves.

See table on next page for more details and comparisons among the Wisteria species.

Prevention & Control—Do not purchase or plant Asian wisterias. Seedlings and young plants can be pulled by hand. To prevent girdling and smothering of trees and to eliminate excess weight, cut vines near the base of the tree. To kill vines including the roots, a systemic herbicide can be applied to freshly cut stems. Long-term control requires commitment because new sprouts can continue to emerge from the root system or grow from seed for several years.

Native Alternatives—American wisteria (*W. frutescens*), which is native to the Coastal Plain in Virginia and further south; coral honeysuckle (*Lonicera sempervirens*); American groundnut (*Apios americana*); trumpet creeper (*Campsis radicans*).

American wisteria

Jil Swearingen

VINES

Wisteria Comparisons

SPECIES	STEM	LEAVES	FLOWERS	FRUIT & SEED
Japanese wisteria *Wisteria floribunda*	Twines *counter-clockwise* (from ground up) Climbs to 70' Stem slender	Leaves with *11–19 leaflets* Leaflets with *wavy margins*, papery thin, oval to lance-shaped, about 1½–3" long by ½" wide	April–July Racemes *8–28" long*, appear *with leaves*; open *progressively* from base to tip; *violet to violet-blue or white*	Pod *velvety pubescent* Seed *round*, *flat*
Chinese wisteria *Wisteria sinensis*	Twines *clockwise* Climbs to 70' Stem stout	Leaves with *7–13 leaflets* Leaflets with *wavy margins*, oval-elliptic to lance-shaped, 2–3 (4)" long by ¾–1½" wide	April–July Racemes *4–13" long*, appear *before leaves*; open *simultaneously*; *pale purple or white*	Pod *velvety pubescent* Seed *round*, *flat*
Hybrid wisteria *Wisteria x formosa*	Twines *counter-clockwise* Climbs to 70'	Leaves with *7–17 leaflets* Leaflets with *wavy margins*	April–July Racemes *4–14" long*, appear *with leaves*; open nearly *simultaneously* or *progressively* from base to tip; *violet or white*	Pod *velvety pubescent* Seed *round*, *flat*
Silky wisteria *Wisteria brachybotrys*	Twines *counter-clockwise* Climbs to 30'	Leaves with *9–13 leaflets* Leaflets covered with *long silky hairs*	May–June Racemes *4–6" long*, appear *with leaves*; open *progressively* from base to tip; *white or pale violet*	Pod *velvety pubescent* Seed *round*, *flat*
American wisteria *Wisteria frutescens* **NATIVE**	Twines *clockwise* Climbs to 50' Stem chestnut brown	Leaves with *5–15 leaflets* Leaflets *dull grayish-green beneath*, straight margins, elliptic to lance-shaped	April–May Racemes *1–6" long*, appear after leaves; open *progressively* from base to tip; *pale purple (or white)*	Pod *smooth* Seed *kidney-shaped*, *not flat*

VINES

OTHER INVASIVE PLANTS

The plants described below are becoming increasingly invasive in natural areas in the mid-Atlantic region. Many of these species are known to be problematic elsewhere in North America and have the potential to become serious invaders here. Documenting new occurrences of invasive species is a crucial first step in Early Detection and Rapid Response (EDRR) and provides distribution data that can help with control and prevention actions. If you spot these invaders in the wild, report them using the Early Detection and Distribution Mapping System (EDDMapS) or iNaturalist.

FORBS

Goutweed

Aegopodium podagraria L. / Parsley family (Apiaceae)

© Judy Fulton

Goutweed, also known as bishop's weed and ground elder, is a perennial, creeping rhizomatous forb native to Europe and temperate portions of Asia that was introduced to North America as an ornamental. It has been reported as invasive in natural areas from Minnesota to Missouri and Maine to Georgia, and in Idaho, Montana, Oregon and Washington. It grows well in moist, shaded areas, forest edges, and various disturbed habitats.

Goutweed spreads by long, white, branching rhizomes (creeping rootstalks) and forms dense patches that push out and exclude native species. The plant has compound leaves divided once or twice into groups of three leaflets, and two leaf forms: **basal leaves** with leafstalks attached to an underground rhizome and **leaves on flowering stalks**. The leaf stalks are long and have sheathed bases. There are "wild" forms with green foliage and cultivated forms with white-margined or variegated leaves. Flowers are tiny, white, and arranged in 2–4½" wide, flat-topped umbels, June-August. Goutweed spreads by seed and rhizomes, including rhizome fragments in yard waste and compost piles. When soil is moist, plants can be hand-pulled gently to extract the rhizomes. The ability of goutweed to regrow readily from rhizomes makes it a challenge to control. A systemic herbicide may be needed to manage large dense infestations.

OTHER INVASIVES

BROADLEAF HELLEBORINE
Epipactis helleborine (L.) Crantz / Orchid family (Orchidaceae)

P.M. Dziuk, MinnesotaWildflowers.info

P.M. Dziuk, MinnesotaWildflowers.info

Broadleaf helleborine is a perennial, herbaceous orchid native to Asia, Europe and northern Africa that was introduced to the U.S. as an ornamental. It has been reported as invasive in natural areas from Minnesota to Arkansas and Maine to Tennessee, and in California, Colorado, Montana, New Mexico, Oregon, and Washington. It is becoming increasingly invasive in the mid-Atlantic region, especially in dry, gravelly soils of forest and woodland edges.

The plant grows to 3' high and has broad, dull green, strongly ribbed leaves that alternate along the stems. Flowers are ½–¾" across, with three petals: the lower petal forms a slipper-like pouch; the two lateral petals are egg-shaped with pointed tips. Petal color varies from pale yellow to green, pink and reddish-purple and petals are usually streaked with darker purple veins. Beneath the petals, and alternating with them, are three pale green to pink, often streaked, sepals. Each inflorescence can be up to 12" tall and contain as many as 50 flowers. The young, drooping inflorescence becomes erect as the buds mature and flower July-August. Although broadleaf helleborine is an orchid, it superficially resembles several native lilies that occur in our region, all with 6 petals and radially symmetrical flowers: Virginia bunchflower (*Veratrum virginicum*), Appalachian bunchflower (*Veratrum parviflorum*) and green false hellebore (*Veratrum viride*). Broadleaf helleborine can be dug up, bagged, and disposed of in a landfill.

Although broadleaf helleborine is an orchid, it superficially resembles several native lilies that occur in our region, all with 6 petals and radially symmetrical flowers: Virginia bunchflower (*Veratrum virginicum*), Appalachian bunchflower (*Veratrum parviflorum*) and green false hellebore (*Veratrum viride*). Broadleaf helleborine can be dug up, bagged, and disposed of in a landfill.

OTHER INVASIVES

GIANT HOGWEED

Heracleum mantegazzianum Sommier & Levier / Parsley family (Apiaceae)

© Bill Johnson

© Bill Johnson

DO NOT TOUCH THIS PLANT. Giant hogweed is a dangerous plant that is designated a federal noxious weed due to toxic sap that increases skin sensitivity to UV radiation, thus causing severe burns.

Giant hogweed is a towering biennial forb native to Europe and Asia that was introduced to the U.S. around 1917 as an ornamental. It has been reported as invasive in natural areas from Wisconsin to Maine and Illinois to New Jersey, in Oregon and Washington, and in North Carolina. It prefers full sun in moist, rich soils in disturbed areas such as riverbanks, ditches and railroad rights-of-way.

Giant hogweed has a large hollow stem up to 6" in diameter and is marked with *purple spots and splotches*. It can grow to an impressive 20' high. Leaves are very large—with *lower leaves to 10' long and over 5½' wide*—alternate, compound with 3–5 deeply lobed leaflets and toothed margins. Flowering occurs late spring to early summer. Flowers are white, very small, and arranged in terminal groups of flattened umbels up to 2½' across. Giant hogweed spreads by seed. It may be confused with the much smaller native *cow parsnip* (*Heracleum sphondylium* ssp. *montanum*) that grows to 6' high and has stems *usually lacking the purple spots and splotches* of giant hogweed.

Do not purchase or plant giant hogweed. Report occurrences to the Department of Agriculture in your state and request assistance with removal.

OTHER INVASIVES

SPANISH BLUEBELLS
Hyacinthoides hispanica (Mill.) Rothm. / Asparagus family (Asparagaceae)

© Bill Johnson

Spanish bluebells (synonyms *Scilla campanulata* and *Scilla hispanica*) is a bulbous, spring-flowering perennial forb native to Spain and Portugal that was introduced as an ornamental. It has been reported as invasive in natural areas in isolated locations in New York, New Jersey, Maryland, Virginia, Georgia, and possibly Delaware. It grows best in some shade in rich, moist, well-drained soil, and poses a threat to native spring-blooming wildflowers already heavily impacted by fig buttercup (*Ficaria verna*), garlic mustard (*Alliaria petiolata*) and other invasives. Spanish bluebells has weak, pale green, strap-shaped basal leaves and nodding, bell-shaped flowers on erect stalks to 18" high. Flower color includes violet-blue, purple, pink and white. Flowering occurs in spring, and plants become dormant by early summer. Spanish bluebells spreads by seed, bulbs, bulb-offsets, and rhizomes, making control difficult. To prevent regrowth, make sure to remove all bulbs and rhizomes when digging up plants.

YELLOW ARCHANGEL
Lamium galeobdolon (L.) L. / Mint family (Lamiaceae)

© Bill Johnson    © Judy Fulton

Yellow archangel (synonym *Lamiastrum galeobdolon*), also known as golden dead-nettle, is a perennial forb native to Europe that was introduced as an ornamental and has been escaping from gardens. It is reported as invasive in natural areas from Minnesota to Maine and Nebraska to Virginia, and in Alabama, California, Oregon, and Washington. Yellow archangel favors wet or moist locations, including floodplains, stream banks, and forests, in full or partial shade, but can also grow among rocks in full sun. It is found in isolated, dense patches, often adjacent to gardens, and displaces native plants.

Yellow archangel grows as an erect perennial forb and sprawling groundcover to 2' tall and, like other mints, has a square stem. Both the stem and leaf stalks are hairy. Leaves are opposite, oval, with toothed margins, and can be green or green with silver splotches. Flowers are yellow, bilaterally symmetrical with 5 fused petals that form an upper hood and a lower lip with reddish lines (nectar guides), arranged in whorls around the stem, and occur April-June. Yellow archangel spreads rapidly by root fragments and seed, especially in fertile soil. Because small root fragments can resprout vigorously, hand-pulling may be ineffective. A dense newspaper and mulch blanket may help control the plant in small areas. Application of a systemic herbicide that kills the entire plant including the roots may be more effective.

SUMMER-SNOWFLAKE
Leucojum aestivum L. / **Amaryllis family (Amaryllidaceae)**

© Bill Johnson

Summer-snowflake is a bulbous perennial forb native to temperate Asia and Europe that was introduced as an ornamental. It has been reported invasive in natural areas from Missouri to Texas and Maine to South Carolina, and in California and Oregon. It is found in moist habitats shared by two entrenched invasives: fig buttercup (*Ficaria verna*) and garlic mustard (*Alliaria petiolata*). Summer snowflake blooms in spring (March-April), not summer, and poses a threat to native spring ephemeral wildflower species. Flowers are nodding and each flower has six white tepals decorated with a small green spot on the outer tip. The species grows to 24' tall and can be confused with other spring-flowering plants with white flowers, such as snowdrop (*Galanthus nivalis*), garden star-of-Bethlehem (*Ornithogalum umbellatum*), and fairy lily (*Zephyranthes candida*). Plants should be dug up, bagged, and disposed of in a landfill.

SHRUBS

BUTTERFLYBUSH

Buddleja davidii **Franch.** / Snapdragon family (Scrophulariaceae)

Butterflybush is native to southwestern China and was introduced to the U.S. around 1900 as an ornamental. It escapes from plantings and has been reported as invasive in natural areas from Michigan to Alabama and Massachusetts to Georgia, as well as in Kansas, California, Oregon, and Washington. It prefers disturbed sites and riparian areas.

Butterflybush is a deciduous shrub with arching stems that can grow to 10' high. The leaves are opposite, pale gray-green, velvety, lance-shaped with toothed margins, and 6–10" long. Flowers are produced in 4–8"-long wand-like clusters at the tips of stems, June–October. Each flower has four fused petals with wavy margins and a deep yellow to orange center. Flower color ranges from dark purple and lilac to pink and white. While butterflybush produces abundant flowers with plentiful nectar that attracts butterflies, it does not serve as a host plant for caterpillars and therefore is a biological dead-end. Spread of butterflybush is mainly through wind-dispersed seed. Young plants can be pulled by hand or uprooted with a shovel. Large plants can be cut down and treated with a systemic herbicide applied to freshly cut stems.

© Judy Fulton

CASTOR-ARALIA

Kalopanax septemlobus **(Thunb.) Koidz.** / Ginseng family (Araliaceae)

Castor-aralia is a deciduous ornamental shade tree native to China, Japan, Korea, and the Russian Federation, that was introduced to the U.S. in 1865. It has been reported as invasive in natural areas in Maryland, Virginia, Connecticut, Illinois, Massachusetts, New Hampshire, New York, and Ohio. It prefers cool, moist climates and is very cold-tolerant. Castor-aralia is found in field and forest margins, tolerates partial to full sun, and grows best in

Robert Vidéki, bugwood.org,

OTHER INVASIVES

deep, moist, fertile, well-drained soil. It can grow to 60' or more high and 30–40' across. Young bark is armed with long, thick spines; mature bark is grayish-brown, deeply furrowed, and typically lacks spines. Leaves are alternate, 7–12" across, palmate (shaped like a hand) with 5–7 lobes, toothed margins, and long leaf stalks. Leaves are dark, glossy green, turning dull yellow to red in fall and resemble castor bean (*Ricinus communis*) leaves. Flowers are tiny, with 4–5 creamy white petals, arranged in small umbels within much larger umbels, July-August. The fruit is a small berry that becomes black in September to October, and occurs in ball-like clusters that persist into winter. Distant spread is by birds and possibly other animals that consume the fruits and expel seeds in new locations. Expelled seeds have a high germination rate. Local spread is by root sprouts and seeds. Young plants can be pulled by hand. Large plants can be extracted using a weed wrench tool or cut and treated with a systemic herbicide.

JETBEAD

Rhodotypos scandens (Thunb.) Makino / Rose family (Rosaceae)

Jil Swearingen

© *Bill Johnson*

Jetbead is a multi-stemmed deciduous shrub that can grow to 6' high. Native to temperate Asia, it was introduced to the U.S. in 1866 as an ornamental. It has been reported as invasive in natural areas from Wisconsin to Alabama and Massachusetts to Georgia, and in Nebraska and Kansas. It is shade-tolerant and grows well in forest interiors where it displaces native plants. Leaves are opposite, 2–4" long by 1–2" wide, with ribbed veins, doubly-toothed margins, and tapering tips. Flowers occur late spring to early summer and are about 1" across, with 4 white petals and 4 green sepals with toothed margins. Up to four shiny, black bead-like fruits, each about 3/10" wide, are produced per flower. Distant spread is by birds and small mammals that consume fruits and expel seeds in new locations. Local spread is by rhizomes, root suckers, and seeds. Hand-pull young plants or uproot large plants using a weed wrench type tool.

OTHER INVASIVES

TREES

AMUR CORKTREE
Phellodendron amurense Rupr. / Rue family (Rutaceae)

© Bill Johnson

Amur corktree is native to China, Japan, Korea, and the Russian Federation and was introduced into the U.S. as an ornamental in 1856. It has been reported as invasive from Minnesota to Missouri and New Hampshire to Virginia. It prefers full sun and rich soils and can form patches that displace native forbs, shrubs and trees.

Amur corktree is dioecious (male and female flowers on separate plants) and can reach 35–45' at maturity. The bark is slightly spongy or corky to the touch and has a distinctive bright neon-yellow inner bark. The light golden brown outer bark of younger trees turns gray-brown and ridged on mature trees. Leaves are opposite, 10–15" long, pinnately compound with 5–11 entire, dark green leaflets that turn bright yellow in the fall. When crushed, the leaves have a distinctive citrusy or turpentine-like smell. Both male and female flowers are yellow-green and occur in drooping panicles in May-June. Female trees produce abundant clusters of bright green fruits (drupes) ¼–½" wide that turn black in July-September. Fruits may remain on the tree into winter. Spread of Amur corktree is by seed. Seedlings can be pulled by hand. Trees will likely need to be cut and treated with a systemic herbicide.

VINES

CHINESE YAM
Dioscorea polystachya Turcz. / Yam family (Dioscoreaceae)

Chinese yam, also known as Chinese-potato and cinnamon-vine, is an herbaceous, deciduous, perennial twining vine native to China that was introduced to the U.S. as an ornamental, medicinal, and food plant. It may have begun escaping cultivation by the mid-1990s. Chinese yam has been reported as invasive in natural areas in two dozen states from Michigan to Vermont, south to Florida, and west to Kansas. It grows in moist soil and full sun to shade in a variety of disturbed habitats, and forms dense tangles of vines that cover and kill native woody and herbaceous plants.

OTHER INVASIVES

Stems are thin, wiry, and twine in a clockwise direction (left to right going upwards). Leaves are simple, 1½–3" long, heart- to arrow-shaped with a deeply lobed base and tapering tip. Chinese yam rarely flowers in the U.S. Reproduction and spread are primarily by small round, potato-like aerial bulbils produced in leaf axils, and by large, elongated, yam-like underground tubers.

© Judy Fulton

Native look-alikes, all lacking aerial bulbils, include **common wild yam** (*Dioscorea villosa*) with rounded heart-shaped leaves and stems that twine in a counter clockwise direction (right to left going upwards); **wild potato-vine** (*Ipomoea pandurata*) with heart- to arrow-shaped leaves and large showy white flowers with purple centers; **small white morning-glory** (*Ipomoea lacunosa*) with heart- to arrow-shaped leaves and small white (sometimes pale purple) flowers; **saw greenbriar** (*Smilax bona-nox*) with heart- to arrow-shaped leaves, thorns and blue to purple berries.

Non-native look-alikes, also lacking bulbils, include **tall morning-glory** (*Ipomoea purpurea*) with heart-shaped leaves and showy purple, deep rose or white flowers with white centers; and **field bindweed** (*Convolvulus arvensis*) with halberd-shaped leaves and white flowers.

Young plants can be pulled by hand or dug up, ensuring that all roots are removed to prevent regrowth. For small infestations, mulching, grubbing, and repeated mowing or cutting can be effective. For large infestations, use of an herbicide applied after leaf expansion and before aerial tubers are ripe may be effective.

Note: Yams are genus *Dioscorea* (yam family, Dioscoreaceae); sweet potatoes are genus *Ipomoea* (morning-glory family, Convolvulaceae); baking potatoes are genus *Solanum* (nightshade family, Solanaceae).

OTHER INVASIVES

CONTROL METHODS

This section provides general guidance on the prevention and management of invasive plants. For more detailed control methods, refer to: Miller et al., *A Management Guide for Invasive Plants in Southern Forests* (2017); Moorhead et al., *A Land Manager's Guide to Best Management Practices (BMPs) to Prevent the Introduction and Spread of Invasive Species* (2011); Penn State Extension, *Invasive and Competing Plants* (2021); and Thompson & Imlay, *Control of Invasive Non-Native Plants: A Guide for Gardeners and Homeowners in the Mid-Atlantic Region* (2011).

PREVENTION

It is everyone's responsibility to help keep potential and known invaders out of our aquatic and terrestrial ecosystems. Once introduced, species with invasive tendencies can become established, spread, cause ecological and economic harm, and threaten human health. Managing invasive species is extremely costly and, in some cases, essentially impossible. The most effective ways to control invasives are to prevent: 1) the importation into the U.S. of known or potentially harmful plants from foreign countries, and 2) the translocation of species from places within the U.S. where they are native to places where they are not. An example of the latter is the intentional introduction of smooth cordgrass (*Spartina alterniflora*), a native of Atlantic and Gulf Coast states, to coastal wetlands in California and Washington (where the species is not native). Smooth cordgrass established and spread, and has become a major invasive plant species, causing significant ecological and economic impacts to West Coast estuaries.

Education—Educating yourself is the first step. Learn how to identify, report, control, and prevent the introduction and establishment of invasive species. The *Mid-Atlantic Invaders Tool* (MAIT) is an excellent resource for current information on invasive animals, plants, and microorganisms in the mid-Atlantic region. By becoming well informed, you are better prepared to take action and share accurate information with others.

Early Detection and Rapid Response (EDRR)—This approach encourages regular monitoring to help find *new invasive species* and *new locations of known invasives*. EDRR is the most cost-effective and proactive tool for dealing with invasive species. If found and documented soon after arriving, a known or potentially invasive species can be removed before it becomes established and unmanageable. Report invasive plants in the wild using the *Early Detection and Distribution Mapping System* (EDDMapS) and associated mobile apps. Reports are checked and verified by participating experts.

Disposal of Invasive Plants—When disposing of pulled plants, place material in sturdy plastic bags and discard in a landfill. If pulled plants are being piled up and left onsite, the area will need to be monitored for new growth in subsequent years. Depending on the species, new plants can grow from seeds, bulbs, tubers, and pieces of stems, roots, and rhizomes.

Prevent Introduction & Spread of Invasive Plants:

- Never purchase, transplant or share invasive plants.
- Never dump unwanted aquatic plants into flowing water or still water connected to flowing water.
- Clean aquatic plant material from boats, motors, and trailers before and after entering water bodies.
- Clean shoes, boots and clothing of mud and seeds when moving from infested to non-infested areas.
- Choose heat-treated mulch, sterilized soil, and certified weed-free hay when purchasing landscape materials.
- Choose plants that are locally native and from reputable growers; avoid mass-produced "native" plants of unknown origin.
- Inspect soil around transplanted plants for unwelcome invasive hitch-hikers.

Management

To effectively manage an invasive species, you need to identify it, understand its biology and habits, investigate the range of control options available, and select the most appropriate method for the particular situation. This approach is referred to as **Integrated Pest Management (IPM)** and was first used in the 1970s by agriculture due to concerns about pesticide overuse. When applied to vegetation management, this approach is referred to as **Integrated Vegetation Management (IVM)**. IPM methods include *biological*, *chemical*, *cultural*, *manual*, and *mechanical*, each with its own set of risks. For example, pruning snips, hatchets, saws, weed whips, and mowers can lead to serious injury if blades are not kept sharp or are used in an unsafe or unintended manner; herbicides can pose risks to the applicator, other people, animals, non-target plants and the environment if not used properly. The goal of IPM is to manage pests in an informed, deliberate, and responsible manner to achieve effective control of targeted species while minimizing risks and harm to people and the environment.

Control Methods

Biological—Biological control is the use of living organisms, most commonly insects and pathogens, to kill or impede the spread of targeted pest plants. The U.S. Department of Agriculture is responsible for review and approval of proposed biological agents, and uses a rigorous process to ensure that they affect only the intended species. Once approved, biological controls can be used by public or private land managers. Biological agents are included in this book if they have been approved for use, are under consideration for approval, or are undergoing research as of 2022. Prior to releasing an approved biocontrol, you will need to contact the USDA to determine whether permits are required.

Chemical—Chemical control involves the use of *herbicides*—pesticides that kill plants. Because it is difficult to precisely direct the herbicide stream and to control droplets drifting through the air (especially during breezy and very hot weather), treatments can damage or kill desirable plants. Before applying any herbicide, make sure you understand the risks of the chemicals, what protective clothes and equipment you need to wear, how to mix and apply the product, and how to dispose of excess mix and concentrate. *Always read the pesticide label and follow all requirements and recommendations to prevent harm to the environment, yourself, and others.* Pesticide certification training, testing, and licensing are provided through state departments of agriculture.

Contact Herbicides. These products kill or damage above-ground plant parts and typically target annual plants and seedlings. Unlike systemic herbicides, contact herbicides are not carried within the plant's vascular system to the roots. Some products (e.g., vinegar-based herbicides) may seem harmless, but they can burn skin and eyes, have negative effects on soil microorganisms, and alter soil acidity.

Systemic Herbicides. These types of pesticides are absorbed by the plant and translocated to the roots by the phloem tissue, killing the entire plant.

Cultural—Cultural practices reduce or prevent the establishment, spread, reproduction, and survival of invasive plants by manipulating environmental conditions. Examples include planting native species to compete with invasives; smothering invasives with thick layers of biodegradable mulch, fabric, and other materials; and employing solarization (i.e., magnifying the heat of the sun) to weaken or kill invasive plants and propagules in upper soil layers.

Manual—Manual control includes hand-pulling and use of pruning snips, hand saws, shovels, weed wrenches, and other non-powered tools. Goats and other grazing animals are also employed for manual control of invasive plants.

Mechanical—Mechanical control includes the use of powered equipment such as chainsaws, weed whackers, mowers, and bush hogs.

GUIDANCE FOR AQUATIC PLANTS

Activities including the sale, purchase, interstate transport, release, and disposal of aquatic plants are regulated by federal and many state laws. In most jurisdictions, permits are required to use pesticides and to remove or install plants in flowing water (e.g., streams and rivers) or in still water (e.g., ponds and ditches) connected to flowing water. However, there are exceptions. In Maryland, a person who owns or rents a pier, dock, or ramp on the Chesapeake Bay or its tributaries may remove SAV in a 60' wide strip, without approval of the Maryland Department of Natural Resources, in order to provide water access. Always check local regulations and consult the appropriate natural resource department in your state for assistance and for permits before taking any actions regarding aquatic plants.

Prevention

The prevention strategies outlined above, including **education** and **EDRR**, are important for aquatic species that can be spread easily to new locations by wildlife and people. Additional preventive measures include:

No release of unwanted aquatic plants—Never release aquatic plants into the wild. They can become established in wetlands, streams, lakes and other natural water bodies and cause significant harm.

Disposal of pulled, unwanted aquatic plants—To dispose of unwanted aquatic vegetation, spread plants in a sunny spot and let them desiccate completely. This method will not kill the seeds of plants like water chestnut. If the piled material will not be monitored in following years, it should be bagged and disposed of in a landfill.

Boat ramp monitoring and boat washing stations—These efforts can be very effective against the spread of aquatic invasive plants. In some locations, people are stationed at boat ramps to inspect boats and trailers for invasive plants, animals and other organisms, before and after watercraft enter a water body. If found, material is removed by power sprayers to prevent spread of invasive species into non-infested lakes and rivers. These programs provide an important opportunity to engage with and educate the public on invasive species.

Management

In the tidal waters of the Chesapeake Bay watershed, resource managers protect all native and non-native submerged aquatic vegetation (SAV) because these plants often provide water quality benefits and habitat for fish, shellfish and waterfowl. Generally, if an initial occurrence of invasive SAV is found in a lake or enclosed water body, managers might try to eradicate it. However, when found in tributaries of the Chesapeake Bay, managers provide the invasive aquatic the same protection as any SAV. Report sightings to the U.S. Geological Survey (USGS) Nonindigenous Aquatic Species database. The potential impacts of SAV management on native aquatic plants and animals must be evaluated carefully before implementing any control. Contact the appropriate local natural resource management agency in your state for assistance and permits before taking any action.

Biological—See p. 162.

Chemical—Effectiveness of herbicides used to manage aquatic vegetation varies with concentration, exposure time, and application in the foliar or water column.

Cultural—Changing growing conditions and invasibility of sites can impede establishment and spread of invasive aquatic plants.

- *Planting native SAV* where invasives have been removed or in areas not yet invaded can help prevent establishment of invasive aquatic plants.
- *Water colorants* used to shade out unwanted aquatic vegetation may be effective in small closed water bodies like ponds and pools.
- *Water drawdowns* are sometimes used during winter to kill unwanted aquatic vegetation by exposing plants to freezing and drying. Results vary by species, site, and season. A major consideration is that all plants and animals in a waterbody—including fish, amphibians and invertebrates—can be killed unless sufficient water is left to support them. Drawdowns are less effective for species like hydrilla that produce cold-resistant tubers, turions, or seeds.

Volunteers pull up two-horned water chestnut and pile plants on tarp for onsite disposal

Manual—Hand-pulling plants is possible for some species and situations, including smaller infestations. A hand-rake can be used but will likely produce many fragments that can further spread the plant.

Mechanical—Boat-mounted harvesters can be used to remove large amounts of aquatic vegetation, but this equipment usually does not remove roots, and the process produces many plant fragments that further spread the vegetation. Harvesting typically needs to be repeated seasonally and yearly as plants regrow.

GUIDANCE FOR TERRESTRIAL PLANTS

Prevention

Preventing the spread of invasive species from infested to non-infested areas should always be a priority. Early control of new infestations decreases the likelihood of establishment and expansion, and significantly reduces the resources needed to manage an established invasive species.

Management

Once an invasive species becomes established, options for controlling it include biological, cultural, manual, mechanical, and chemical methods. The advantages and disadvantages of each must be weighed when choosing the best method for a particular situation. Other considerations include the extent of the infestation, habitat and environmental conditions, and availability of resources. Sometimes, combining methods, such as cutting followed by herbicide application, may be more effective.

HERBACEOUS PLANTS
Grasses, Sedges, Forbs & Herbaceous Vines

Control of herbaceous invasives can be challenging because they often grow in large patches mixed with desirable native plants, making it difficult to remove invasive plants without harming native species.

Biological—See p. 162.

Chemical—Chemical options include contact herbicides that kill above-ground parts and systemic herbicides that enter the vascular system and kill the entire plant including the roots. Grass-specific herbicides can be used to control invasive grasses while avoiding damage to broadleaf plants.

Cultural—Cultural control methods for herbaceous invasives include:

- ***Changing soil moisture, soil acidity and light availability*** to make conditions less favorable for invasive species.
- ***Removing flowers and fruits*** to prevent spread by seed.
- ***Smothering plants with mulch*** (e.g., 3–12" of mulch or 3" of mulch on cardboard or newspaper) to prevent regrowth.
- ***Solarizing by securing tough plastic or airtight fabric over plants*** for several months during hot weather to kill or weaken above-ground parts, root crowns, seedlings, and seeds in the top 2" of soil.
- ***Using prescribed burning*** (for species shown to be effectively controlled by prescribed fire) to kill invasives directly and to reduce leaf litter buildup.

CONTROL METHODS

Manual—Manual methods include hand-pulling and the use of non-powered tools to extract invasives. In addition to being labor and time-intensive, other drawbacks include *soil disturbance*—which can bring invasive seeds to the surface—and *creation of open ground* that can become invaded. When hand-pulling, remove the entire plant, including the roots, to prevent regrowth. Pulling works best when the soil is moist. For plants with strong roots, a weed wrench-type tool may be needed to extract the whole plant.

Mechanical—Mechanical methods such as mowing and bush-hogging may be effective for large infestations of herbaceous invasives, including perennials with extensive root systems. When mowed (or bitten off by a grazing animal), grasses regrow quickly from meristematic tissue inside the crowns near the soil surface. Because cutting of running bamboos encourages spread via underground rhizomes, it needs to be combined with herbicide treatment. Consider timing and height of mowing to avoid harm to native animals, especially frogs, turtles, and ground-nesting birds.

WOODY PLANTS
Shrubs, Trees & Woody Vines

Most invasive shrubs, trees and vines need to be completely removed or killed to prevent regrowth from roots. While cultural, manual, and mechanical methods are available, chemical control is sometimes the most effective option, especially for woody plants with extensive root systems and a propensity to resprout.

Biological—See p. 162.

Chemical—Control of established invasive shrubs, trees and vines usually requires the use of a systemic herbicide to kill the entire plant including the roots. The amount of herbicide used can be greatly reduced by using basal bark, cut stem and hack-and-squirt methods. Adding a blue dye to the herbicide mix can help track treatments and avoid repeat applications.

- **Basal bark** treatment is typically used for shrubs, trees and detached woody vines less than about 6" in diameter. A concentrated systemic herbicide is applied in a band around the base of the trunk. This method uses a small amount of herbicide mixture and is generally effective year-round as long as the ground is not frozen.

- **Cut-stem** treatment can be used to control invasive trees. Once the trunk is cut, concentrated systemic herbicide is applied to the freshly cut surface, targeting the outer ring of the cut surface containing the sapwood. The chemical is carried to the roots by the phloem. Cut-stem treatments can be made from full leaf-out through early winter but may be most successful from mid to late summer

through fall when plants are shifting resources to the roots. Dormant season applications may prevent resprouting from the stump, but may not inhibit root-suckering.
- **Hack-and-squirt** treatment is typically used for trees with trunk diameters of 1" or more. Stems less than 1" diameter can be cut or broken and the stubs sprayed with the herbicide mixture. A hatchet or hand axe is used to make downward-angled cuts around a tree trunk, at a convenient height, below the last live branch. Cuts should be about 2" long, spaced 1–2" apart, made one per inch of diameter, penetrate through the bark into the living tissue or sapwood, and create a cupping effect. A small amount of concentrated systemic herbicide (e.g., 1 ml) is dispensed into the cut using a spray bottle, taking care to avoid run-off. A dye can be used to allow the applicator to see treated stems from a distance. This method is particularly effective for killing tree-of-heaven (*Ailanthus altissimus*), which resprouts vigorously if cut down or girdled.
- **Foliar** treatment involves spraying herbicide mixture onto the leaves and requires larger volumes of herbicide than stem treatments. Because foliar applications are made over large areas and desirable plants may be killed or damaged, extra care must be taken to avoid non-target effects. Avoid applications during breezy or hot conditions.

Cultural—Woody plants and seedlings can be smothered by covering them with 3–12" of mulch or 3" of mulch on cardboard or newspaper.

Manual—
- **Hand-pulling** is an effective method for removing many young woody plants and their roots. Seedlings and small plants are easiest to remove when the soil is moist. Pull plants as soon as they are large enough to grasp and ideally before they produce seeds. For most species, the entire root system needs to be removed to avoid resprouting.
- **Grubbing** involves removing woody plants using a pulaski (a double-sided tool with an axe and an adze), weed wrench or similar tool. Try to remove the entire plant, including all roots and runners, to prevent resprouting.
- **Girdling** (i.e., stripping bark and vascular tissue in a circle around a trunk) can be effective for controlling woody invasives but is not recommended for plants that resprout heavily.

Mechanical—
- **Cutting** shrubs, trees, and vines with a chain saw can be effective but may lead to resprouting in some species. When cutting vines that reach high into the tree canopy, avoid pulling on attached vines that may cause heavy branches to fall.
- **Mowing and bush-hogging** are effective for low-growing woody invasives but may need to be repeated and can result in extensive damage to soil.

NATIVE PLANTS FOR LANDSCAPES

Choosing Native Plants—The following pages provide a selection of native plants for use in mid-Atlantic landscapes. These grasses, sedges, ferns, forbs, shrubs, trees and vines are just a starting point; there are hundreds of other species available. Buying local ecotypes and avoiding non-native plants and cultivars (that have been altered through hybridization and selection), will ensure the best support for native wildlife and biodiversity. Use plants that are native to the ecoregion where you live.

Snowberry clearwing caterpillar (*Hemaris diffinis*) feeding on coral honeysuckle (*Lonicera sempervirens*)

Jil Swearingen

Supporting the Web of Life—Do you love birds, butterflies, moths, turtles, frogs, fish and other wildlife? Native animals require native plants to survive and thrive. Native plants are the basis of complex food webs unique to each ecological community. Most insects are *specialists*: they have co-evolved with and are tightly adapted to a small number of plant species for survival; the rest are *generalists* and are biologically compatible with a wide range of plant species.

Most Insects are Plant Specialists

According to researchers, *90 percent of herbivorous (plant-feeding) insects are specialists that can only feed on one or a few plant lineages*. Douglas Tallamy has found that, within the same genus, introduced plant species provide about 68 percent less food for insects than native plants. In other words, caterpillars, which serve as a critical source of bird food, are abundant on native plants, but are rare to non-existent on most non-native species. The nestlings of chickadees, nuthatches, titmice, warblers and other native songbirds each require thousands of protein-rich caterpillars and other insects in order to survive to fledging.

Landscapes dominated by non-native plants do not produce the essential high-protein insect food for breeding birds or the nutritious fruits needed by birds that migrate long distances: these sites might look pretty, but they are biological wastelands. Most songbird species are experiencing precipitous declines in numbers. To help keep these birds on the planet—as well as in our yards—it is critical that we provide the native plants that produce the food birds need to survive.

Douglas Tallamy

A black-throated blue warbler rears its young on moths and caterpillars

Determining Plant Nativity. There are many definitions of "native" used by gardeners, landscapers and nurseries. To plant the most appropriate species, it is important to understand what this term really means and to avoid broad definitions. Some plants and seed mixes are labeled "native," but the label does not specify where these materials are actually native. Some seed mixes include species that are native to many different areas of the U.S. and North America and should be avoided. Use seed mixes that contain only those species native to your ecoregion. Examples of some plants that are commonly sold or marketed incorrectly as "native" include:

- **California poppy (*Eschscholzia californica*)** is native to California, Oregon, Washington, Nevada, Arizona, New Mexico, and northern Mexico, but *not* to the mid-Atlantic.
- **Hubricht's blue-star (*Amsonia hubrichtii*)** is native to Oklahoma and Arkansas, but *not* to the mid-Atlantic.
- **Eastern larch (*Larix laricina*)** is native to some mid-Atlantic mountain regions, but *not* to the mid-Atlantic Coastal Plain.

Finding Native Plants—In response to surging demand for native plants, native plant nurseries have been increasing in number and production capacity. Support these nurseries in your area and request local ecotypes that are genetically adapted to your ecoregion.

NATIVE PLANTS

Grasses

Bottlebrush Grass
Elymus hystrix

© Bill Johnson

Indian Grass
Sorghastrum nutans

© Judy Fulton

© Judy Fulton

Purpletop
Tridens flavus

Wayne Longbottom

Poverty Oatgrass
Danthonia spicata

© Judy Fulton

NATIVE PLANTS

170

Sedges

Woolgrass
Scirpus cyperinus

© Judy Fulton

Blue Wood Sedge
Carex glaucodea

© Judy Fulton

Star Sedge
Carex radiata

© Judy Fulton

Lurid Sedge
Carex lurida

© Judy Fulton

Ferns

Cinnamon Fern
Osmundastrum cinnamomeum

© Judy Fulton

Fancy Fern & Marginal Wood Fern
Dryopteris intermedia & D. marginalis

© Judy Fulton

© Judy Fulton

Ebony Spleenwort
Asplenium platyneuron

© Judy Fulton

Christmas Fern
Polystichum acrostichoides

© Judy Fulton

172

Forbs

New York Ironweed
Vernonia noveborascensis

© Judy Fulton

Wild Columbine
Aquilegia canadensis

© Bill Johnson

© Judy Fulton

Spotted Bee Balm
Monarda punctata

Jil Swearingen

Woodland Stonecrop
Sedum ternatum

© Judy Fulton

NATIVE PLANTS

Forbs

Woodland Phlox
Phlox divaricata

© Judy Fulton

Golden Ragwort
Packera aurea

© Judy Fulton

© Judy Fulton

White Wood Aster
Eurybia divaricata

© Judy Fulton

Foamflower
Tiarella cordifolia

© Judy Fulton

FORBS

Cardinal Flower
Lobelia cardinalis

© Judy Fulton

Wild Ginger
Asarum canadense

© Judy Fulton

© Judy Fulton

Hollow Joe-Pyeweed
Eutrochium fistulosum

© Bill Johnson

Blazing Star
Liatris spicata

© Bill Johnson

NATIVE PLANTS

Forbs

Blue Mistflower
Conoclinum coelestinium

Jil Swearingen

American Alumroot
Heuchera americana

© Judy Fulton

© Judy Fulton

Wreath Goldenrod
Solidago caesia

© Judy Fulton

Solomon's Plume
Maianthemum racemosum

© Judy Fulton

Shrubs

Lowbush Blueberry
Vaccinium angustifolium

© Judy Fulton

Witch Hazel
Hamamelis virginiana

© Bill Johnson

© Judy Fulton

Silky Dogwood
Cornus amomum

© Bill Johnson

Winterberry Holly
Ilex verticillata

Dioecious

Amanda Wray

Native Plants

Shrubs

Shrubby St. John's Wort
Hypericum prolificum

© Judy Fulton

Mountain Laurel
Kalmia latifolia

© Judy Fulton

© Judy Fulton

Sweet Pepperbush
Clethra alnifolia

© Judy Fulton

Purple-Flowering Raspberry
Rubus odoratus

© Bill Johnson

NATIVE PLANTS

Shrubs

Sweet Fern
Comptonia peregrina

© Bill Johnson

Ninebark
Physocarpus opulifolius

Jil Swearingen

Jil Swearingen

New Jersey Tea
Ceanothus americanus

© Judy Fulton

Fringetree
Chionanthus virginicus

Dioecious

Jil Swearingen

NATIVE PLANTS

SHRUBS

Spicebush
Lindera benzoin

© Judy Fulton

Dioecious

Smooth Sumac & Aromatic Sumac
Rhus glabra & R. aromatica

© Judy Fulton

© Bill Johnson

Red Chokeberry
Aronia arbutifolia

Jil Swearingen

© Judy Fulton

Inkberry
Ilex glabra

Dioecious

© Bill Johnson

NATIVE PLANTS

Shrubs

Buttonbush
Cephalanthus occidentalis

© Judy Fulton

American Hazelnut
Corylus americana

© Bill Johnson

© Bill Johnson

American Strawberry Bush
Euonymus americanus

Jil Swearingen

Northern Bayberry
Morella pennsylvanica

Dioecious

© Bill Johnson

Native Plants

Trees

Black Cherry
Prunus serotina

Jil Swearingen

Redbud
Cercis canadensis

Amanda Wray

Jil Swearingen

Sassafras
Sassafras albidum

© Bill Johnson

Willow Oak
Quercus phellos

© Bill Johnson

NATIVE PLANTS

Trees

Virginia Pine
Pinus virginiana

© Bill Johnson

Ironwood
Carpinus caroliniana

© Judy Fulton

© Judy Fulton

Pignut Hickory
Carya glabra

Amanda Wray

Jil Swearingen

Canadian Serviceberry
Amelanchier canadensis

Thomas Palmer

Native Plants

183

TREES

White Oak
Quercus alba

© Bill Johnson

Sweetbay Magnolia
Magnolia virginiana

© Bill Johnson

© Bill Johnson

Sweetgum
Liquidambar styraciflua

© Bill Johnson

American Sycamore
Platanus occidentalis

Amanda Wray

NATIVE PLANTS

184

Trees

Black Gum
Nyssa sylvatica

Dioecious

© Bill Johnson

Eastern Hop Hornbeam
Ostrya virginiana

© Bill Johnson

© Bill Johnson

American Beech
Fagus grandifolia

© Bill Johnson

© Bill Johnson

Black Walnut
Juglans nigra

© Bill Johnson

NATIVE PLANTS

185

Vines

Trumpet Creeper
Campsis radicans

© Judy Fulton

American Groundnut
Apios americana

Jil Swearingen

© Judy Fulton

Wild Yam
Dioscorea villosa

© Judy Fulton

© Bill Johnson

Virginia Virgin's Bower
Clematis virginiana

© Bill Johnson

Native Plants

Vines

Yellow Passionflower
Passiflora lutea

Wayne Longbottom

Coral Honeysuckle
Lonicera sempervirens

© Judy Fulton

Canada Moonseed
Menispermum canadense

© Bill Johnson

Virginia Creeper
Parthenocissus quinquefolia

© Bill Johnson

NATIVE PLANTS

References

Allan, B.F., H.P. Dutra, L.S. Goessling, K. Barnett, J.M. Chase, R.J. Marquis, G. Pang, G.A. Storch, R.E. Thach and J.L. Orrock. 2010. Invasive honeysuckle eradication reduces tick-borne disease risk by altering host dynamics. Proceedings of the National Academy of Sciences, USA 107(43):18523- 18527.

Atha, D., J.A. Schuler and S. Lumban Tobing. 2014. *Corydalis incisa* (Fumariaceae) in Bronx and Westchester counties, New York. Phytoneuron 96:1–6.

Baisden, E.C., D.W. Tallamy, D.L. Narango and E. Boyle. 2018. D o cultivars of native plants support insect Herbivores? Hort Technology 28(5):596–606.

Bargeron, C. and J. Swearingen. 2018. Invasive Plant Atlas of the United States. Center for Invasive Species and Ecosystem Health, University of Georgia.

Batcher, M.S. and S.A. Stiles. 2000. Element Stewardship Abstract for *Lonicera maackii* (Rupr.) Maxim (Amur honeysuckle), *Lonicera morrowii* A. Gray (Morrow's honeysuckle), *Lonicera tatarica* L. (Tatarian honeysuckle), *Lonicera* x *bella* Zabel (Bell's honeysuckle): The Bush honeysuckles. Global Invasive Species Team, The Nature Conservancy. 11 pp.

Bender, J. and J. Rendall. 1987. Element Stewardship Abstract for *Lythrum salicaria*, Purple Loosestrife. The Nature Conservancy. 10 pp.

Bickley, W.E. and E.N. Cory. 1955. Water caltrop in the Chesapeake Bay. Association of Southeastern Biologists Bulletin 2:27–28.

Bossard, C.C., J.M. Randall and M.C. Hoshovsky (Editors). 2000. Invasive Plants of California's Wildlands. University of California Press, Berkeley, CA. 360 pp.

Bradley, B.A., E.M. Beaury, E.J. Fusco, B.J. Griffin, B.B. Laginhas, B. C. McLaughlin and L. Munro. 2019. Regional Invasive Species & Climate Change Management Challenge: Double Trouble. Understanding risks from invasive species + climate change. Northeast RISCC Management, University of Massachusetts, Amherst, MA.

Brown, R.G. and M.L. Brown. 1972. Woody Plants of Maryland. Port City Press. Baltimore, MD. 347 pp.

Brown, R.G. and M.L. Brown. 1984. Herbaceous Plants of Maryland. Port City Press. Baltimore, MD. 1127 pp.

Burgess, K.S. and B.C. Husband. 2006. Habitat differentiation and the ecological costs of hybridization: the effects of introduced mulberry (*Morus alba*) on a native congener (*M. rubra*). Journal of Ecology 94(6):1061–1069.

California Academy of Sciences and the National Geographic Society. iNaturalist. Accessed 2022.

Casagrande, R.A. and J.E. Dacey. 2007. Monarch butterfly oviposition on swallow-worts (*Vincetoxicum* spp.). Environmental Entomology 36(3):631–636.

Cech, R. and G. Tudor. 2007. Butterflies of the East Coast: An Observer's Guide. Princeton University Press, Princeton, NJ. 360 pp.

Chayka, Katy. Minnesota Wildflowers, a field guide to the flora of Minnesota. Accessed 2022.

Chorak, G.M., L.L. Dodd, N. Rybicki, K. Ingram, M. Buyukyoruk, Y. Kadono, Y.Y. Chen and R.A. Thum. 2019. Cryptic introduction of water chestnut (*Trapa*) in the northeastern United States. Aquatic Botany 155:32–37.

Cipollini, D., R. Stevenson, S. Enright, A. Eyles and P. Bonello. 2008. Phenolic metabolites in leaves of the invasive shrub, Lonicera maackii, and their potential phytotoxic and anti-herbivore effects. Journal of C hemical Ecology 34:144–52.

Coffey, S. 2021. Italian Arum: A "Dirty Dozen" Plant. Lewis Ginter Botanical Garden.
Coffey, S. 2021. Mulberry Weed: A "Dirty Dozen" Plant. Lewis Ginter Botanical Garden.

Crowl, T.A., T.O. Crist, R.R. Parmenter, G. Belovsky and A.E. Lugo. 2008. The spread of invasive species and infectious disease as drivers of ecosystem change. Ecological Society of America, Frontiers in Ecology and the Environment 6(5):238–246.

Culley, T.M. and N.A. Hardiman. 2007. The beginning of a new invasive plant: a history of the ornamental Callery pear in the United States. Oxford University Press on behalf of the American Institute of Biological Sciences. BioScience 57(11):956-964.

Cummings, D.C., T.G. Bidwell, C.R. Medlin, S.D. Fuhlendorf, R.D. Elmore and J.R. Weir. 2017. Ecology and Management of Sericea Lespedeza, NREM-2874. Oklahoma State University Extension, Stillwater, OK. 7 pp.

Czarapata, E.J. 2005. Invasive Plants of the Upper Midwest: An Illustrated Guide to Their Identification and Control. The University of Wisconsin Press, Madison, WI. 236 pp.

Delaware Native Plant Society. 2002. Delaware Native Plants for Landscaping and Restoration: Recommended Species for the Property Owner and Land Steward. 19 pp.

Denchak, M. 2022. Natural Resources Defense Council: How you can stop global warming. Natural Resources Defense Council, New York, NY.

Dingwell, S. 2014. Unwanted and Unloved: Porcelain-berry! Virginia Native Plant Society.

Dirr, M.A. 2009. Manual of Woody Landscape Plants: Their Identification, Ornamental Characteristics, Culture, Propagation and Uses, 6th Ed. Stipes Publishing, LLC, Champaign, IL. 1325 pp.

DiTomaso, J.M. and E.A. Healy. 2003. Aquatic and Riparian Weeds of the West, Publ. No. 3421. University of California, Division of Agriculture and Natural Resources. Oakland, CA. 442 pp.

DiTomaso, J.M. and E.A. Healy. 2007. Weeds of California and Other Western States, Vol. 1 and 2, Publ. No. 3488. University of California, Division of Agriculture and Natural Resources. Oakland, CA. 1808 pp.

DiTommaso, A., F.M. Lawlor and S.J. Darbyshire. 2005. The biology of invasive alien plants in Canada. 2. *Cynanchum rossicum* (Kleopow) Borhidi [= *Vincetoxicum rossicum* (Kleopow) Barbar.] and *Cynanchum louiseae* (L.) Kartesz & Gandhi [= *Vincetoxicum nigrum* (L.) Moench]. Canadian Journal of Plant Science 85(1):243–263.

Dodd, L.L. and A.N. Schad. 2021. Evaluation of light limitation and depth on germinated seeds of two species of water chestnut cultured under experimental conditions. Aquatic Plant Control Research Program Technical Note ERDC/TN APCRP-CC-23. U.S. Army Corps of Engineers, Engineer Research and Development Center, Vicksburg, MS. 12 pp.

Dodd, L.L., N.B. Rybicki, R.A. Thum, Y. Kadono and K. Ingram. 2019. Genetic and morphological differences of water chestnut (Myrtales:Lythraceae:Trapa) populations in the Northeastern United States, Japan, and South Africa. Aquatic Plant Control Research Program, Environmental Laboratory, Technical Reports Collection ERDC/EL TR-19-3. U.S. Army Corps of Engineers, Engineer Research and Development Center, Vicksburg, MS. 45 pp.

Dodd, L.L., N.E. Harms and A.N. Schad. 2021. Reciprocal competitive effects of congeneric invaders, *Trapa natans* L. and *Trapa bispinosa* Roxb. var. *iinumai* Nakano, in established freshwater plant cultures. Aquatic Botany 174:103419.

Ehrenfeld, J.G., P. Kourtev and W. Huang. 2001. Changes in soil functions following invasions of exotic understory plants in deciduous forests. Ecological Applications 11(5):1287–1300.

Ellis, K. 2013. Identifying and promoting pollinator-rewarding herbaceous perennial plant species. Final Report to Pennsylvania Department of Agriculture. 16 pp.

Falconi, D. 2015. Foraging & Feasting: A Field Guide and Wild Food Cookbook. Botanical Arts Press, Accord, NY. 240 pp.

Fernald, M.L. 1950. Gray's Manual of Botany: A Handbook of the Flowering Plants and Ferns of the Central and Northeastern United States and Adjacent Canada, 8th Ed. American Book Company, New York, NY. 1632 pp.

Fofonoff, P.W., G.M. Ruiz, B. Steves, A.H. Hines and J.T. Carlton. National Exotic Marine and Estuarine Species Information System (NEMESIS): Chesapeake Bay Introduced Species Database. Access 2022.

Forest Health Staff. 2005. Weed of the Week: Beefsteak plant, *Perilla frutescens* (L.) Britt. USDA Forest Service, Newtown Square, PA.

Fryer, J.L. 2010. Ailanthus altissima. In: Fire Effects Information System. U.S. Department of Agriculture, Forest Service, Rocky Mountain Research Station, Fire Sciences Laboratory (Producer).

Fryer, J.L. 2010. Albizia julibrissin. In: Fire Effects Information System. U.S. Department of Agriculture, Forest Service, Rocky Mountain Research Station, Fire Sciences Laboratory (Producer).

Fryer, J.L. 2011. Celastrus orbiculatus. In: Fire Effects Information System, U.S. Department of Agriculture, Forest Service, Rocky Mountain Research Station, Fire Sciences Laboratory (Producer).

Fulton, J. and S. Tangren. 2022. Don't Jump to Conclusions about Asian Jumpseed; Invader of the Month: Asian jumpseed—*Persicaria filiformis*. Maryland Invasive Species Council.

Fulton, J.P., J.M. Swearingen and C.T. Bargeron. Mid-Atlantic Invaders Tool (MAIT). University of Georgia, Center for Invasive Species and Ecosystem Health, Tifton, GA. Access 2022.

Gassmann, A., A. Weed, L. Tewksbury, A. Leroux, S. Smith, R. Dejonge, R. Bourchier and R. Casagrande. 2011. Evaluating the potential for biological control of swallow-worts (Vincetoxicum nigrum and V. rossicum) in eastern North America. XIII Symposium on Biological Control of Weeds. Pre-Release Testing of Weed Biological Control Agents, Session 1:45.

Gleason, H.A. and A. Cronquist. 1991. Manual of Vascular Plants of Northeastern United States and Adjacent Canada, 2nd Ed. The New York Botanical Garden, Bronx, NY. 910 pp.

Haller, W.T., J.L. Miller and L.A. Garrard. 1976. Seasonal production and germination of Hydrilla vegetative propagules. Journal of Aquatic Plant Management 14:26–29.

Harmon, E. 2006. Japanese Barberry (*Berberis thunbergii*). Introduced Species Summary Project, Columbia University.

Hayden, W.J. 2021. Wildflower of the year 2021 American wisteria (Wisteria frutescens). Virginia Native Plant Society.

Hayden, W.J. 2021. How to know the species of wisteria. Sempervirens, The Quarterly of the Virginia Native Plant Society Summer 2021:4–5.

Hilty, J. 2020. Illinois Wildflowers.

Holloran, P., A. Mackenzie, S. Farrell and D. Johnson. 2004. Weed Workers Handbook: A Guide to Techniques for Removing Bay Area Invasive Plants. The Watershed Project, Richmond, CA, and California Invasive Plant Council, Berkeley, CA. 120 pp.

Holmgren, N.H., P.K. Holmgren and H.A. Gleason. 1998. Illustrated Companion to Gleason and Cronquist's Manual: Illustrations of the Vascular Plants of Northeastern United States and Adjacent Canada. The New York Botanical Garden, Bronx, NY. 937 pp.

Homer, J., A. Decker and S. Bien. 2010. Occurrence of *Schoenoplectus mucronatus* at the U.S. Department of Energy Fernald Preserve. Fernald Preserve, Hamilton, OH. Environmental Science, 2 pp.

Huebner, C.D., C. Olson and H.C. Smith. 2005. Invasive Plants Field and Reference Guide: An Ecological Perspective of Plant Invaders of Forests and Woodlands, NA-TP-05-04. U.S. Department of Agriculture, Forest Service, Northeastern Area State & Private Forestry, Morgantown, WV. 86 pp.

Hummel, M. and E. Kiviat. 2004. Review of world literature on water chestnut with implications for management in North America. Journal of Aquatic Plant Management 42:17–28.

International Dark-Sky Association. Access 2022.

Jackson, D.R. and J.C. Finley. 2019. Using Hack-and-Squirt Herbicide Applications to Control Unwanted Trees. Penn State Extension. 29 pp.

Jackson, D.R. 2022. Invasive Shrub Control. Penn State Extension. 3 pp.

Kalisz S., S.N. Kivlin and L. Bialic-Murphy. 2021. Allelopathy is pervasive in invasive plants. Biological Invasions 23:367–371.

Kartesz, J.T. 2015. The Biota of North America Program (BONAP). Taxonomic Data Center, Chapel Hill, N.C. [maps generated from Kartesz, J.T. 2015. Floristic Synthesis of North America, Version 1.0. Biota of North America Program (BONAP). (in press)].

Kaufmann, S.R. and W. Kaufmann. 2012. *Invasive Plants:* Guide to Identification and the Impacts and Control of Common North American Species, 2nd Ed. Stackpole Books, Mechanicsburg, PA. 518 pp.

Kawahara, A.Y., L.E. Reeves, J.R. Barber and S.H. Black. 2021.Eight simple actions that individuals can take to save insects from global declines. Opinion, Biological Sciences. Proceedings of the National Academy of Sciences of the United States of America 118(2):1–6.

Kew Royal Botanical Gardens, UK. *Fatoua villosa* (Thunb.) Nakai. Plants of the World Online. Access 2022.

Koop, A. 2017. Weed Risk Assessment for *Corydalis incisa* (Thunb.) Pers. (Papaveraceae)—Incised fumewort, Version 1. Plant Protection and Quarantine (PPQ), Animal and Plant Health Inspection Service, U.S. Department of Agriculture, Raleigh, NC. 32 pp.

Kourtev, P.S., J.G. Ehrenfeld and M. Häggblom. 2002. Exotic plant species alter the microbial community structure and function in the soil. Ecological Society of America, Journal of Ecology 83(11):3152-3166.

Kunii, H. 1998. Longevity and germinability of buried seeds in *Trapa* sp. Memoirs of the Faculty of Science, Shimane University, Shimane, Japan 22:83–91.

Lake Restoration Incorporated. Aquatic Plant Management: Hydrilla control. Rogers, MN. Access 2022.

Langeland, K.A. 1996. *Hydrilla verticillata* (L.F.) Royle, Hydrocharitaceae, "The Perfect Aquatic Weed." Castanea, Southern Appalachian Botanical Society 61(3):293–304.

Leckie, S. and D. Beadle. 2018. Peterson Field Guide to Moths of Southeastern North America (Peterson Field Guides). Houghton Mifflin Harcourt, USA. 664 pp.

Les, D.H. 2018. Aquatic Dicotyledons of North America: Ecology, Life History, and Systematics, 1st Ed. CRC Press, Taylor & Francis Group, Boca Raton, FL. 1350 pp.

Les, D.H. 2020. Aquatic Monocotyledons of North America: Ecology, Life History, and Systematics, 1st Ed. CRC Press, Taylor & Francis Group, Boca Raton, FL. 568 pp.

Lilla, E. 2019. Intern Post: Pull out garlic mustard for sure. But cooking with it may be the best revenge. Matthaei Botanical Gardens and Nichols Arboretum, University of Michigan, Ann Arbor, MI.

Magee, D.W. 1981. Freshwater Wetlands: A Guide to Common Indicator Plants of the Northeast. University of Massachusetts Press, Amherst, MA. 240 pp.

Maine Natural Areas Program. Maine Invasive Plants: Variable-Leaf Milfoil, *Myriophyllum heterophyllum* (Water Milfoil Family), Bulletin #2530. Maine Natural Areas Program, Department of Conservation, Augusta, ME, and University of Maine Cooperative Extension, Orono, ME. 2 pp. Access 2022.

Marble, S.C. and S.T. Steed. Biology and management of mulberry weed (*Fatoua villosa*) in ornamental crop production, Publication ENH1256. 2015, revised 2018 & 2022. Environmental Horticulture Department, Mid-Florida Research and Education Center, Apopka (MREC), UF/IFAS Extension, University of Florida.

Matthews, E.R., J.P. Schmit and P. Campbell. 2016. Climbing vines and forest edges affect tree growth and mortality in temperate forests of the U.S. Mid-Atlantic States. Forest Ecology and Management 374:166–173.

Mayfield, A.E. *et al.* 2021. Impacts of invasive species in terrestrial and aquatic systems in the United States. pp 5-39. In: Poland, T.M., T. Patel-Weynand, D.M. Finch, C.F. Miniat, D.C. Hayes, V.M. Lopez. (Editors) Invasive Species in Forests and Rangelands of the United States: A Comprehensive Science Synthesis for the United States Forest Sector. U.S. Department of Agriculture, Forest Service, Northern Research Station. Springer International Publishing, Heidelberg, Germany. 455 pp.

McGowan-Stinski, J. and T. Gostomski. 2005. Recommended removal methods for spotted knapweed (*Centaurea maculosa*). The Nature Conservancy, Michigan Chapter. Grand Rapids, MI. 3 pp.

McKnight, B.N. (Editor). 1993. Biological Pollution: The Control and Impact of Invasive Exotic Species: Proceedings of a Symposium Held at the University Place Conference Center, 1st Ed. Indiana Academy of Science, Indianapolis, IN. 261 pp.

McMahon, G., S.M. Gregonis, S.W. Waltman, J.M. Omernik, T.D. Thorson, J.A. Freeouf, A.H. Rorick and J.E. Keys. 2001. Developing a spatial framework of common ecological regions for the conterminous United States. Environmental Management 28(3):293–316.

Meadows, R.E. and K. Saltonstall. 2007. Distribution of native and introduced Phragmites australis in freshwater and oligohaline tidal marshes of the Delmarva Peninsula and southern New Jersey. The Journal of the Torrey Botanical Society 134(1):99–107.

Meyer, M.H. 2003. *Miscanthus*: Ornamental and Invasive Grass. Minnesota Landscape Arboretum, Chanhassen, MN. 68 pp.

Miller, J.H., E.B. Chambliss and N.J. Loewenstein. 2015. A Field Guide for the Identification of Invasive Plants in Southern Forests, GTR-SRS—119. U.S. Department of Agriculture, Forest Service, Southern Research Station, Ashville, NC. 126 pp.

Miller, J.H., S.T. Manning and S.F. Enloe. 2015. A Management Guide for Invasive Plants in Southern Forests, GTR-SRS-131. U.S. Department of Agriculture, Forest Service, Southern Research Station, Ashville, NC. 120 pp.

Miller K.M., B.J. McGill, A.S. Weed, C.E. Seirup, J.A. Comiskey, E.R. Matthews, S. Perles and J.P. Schmit. 2020. Long-term trends indicate that invasive plants are pervasive and increasing in eastern national parks. Ecological Applications, Ecological Society of America 31(2).

Mirick, P.G. 1996. Goose grief. Massachusetts Wildlife 46(2):15–16.

Missouri Botanical Garden Plant Finder. *Celastrus scandens*. Missouri Botanical Garden, St. Louis, MO. Access 2022.

Natural Resources Conservation Service. Brush Management—Invasive Plant Control, Multiflora Rose—*Rosa multiflora*, Conservation Practice Job Sheet, NH-314. 3 pp. Access 2022.

NatureServe and National Geographic Society. LandScope America: The Conservation Guide to America's Natural Places. Access 2022.

Neal, J. 2016. Mulberryweed (*Fatoua villosa*). Horticulture Information Leaflets. North Carolina State Extension, NC State University and NC A&T State University.

Netherland, M.D. 1997. Turion ecology of Hydrilla. Journal of Aquatic Plant Management 35:1–10.

New Jersey Invasive Species Strike Team. Chinese Yam (Dioscorea polystachya). Plants, Invasive Species Fact Sheets. Friends of Hopewell Valley Open Space (FoHVOS), Pennington, NJ. Access 2022.

New Jersey Invasive Species Strike Team. Linden viburnum (Viburnum dilatatum). Plants, Invasive Species Fact Sheets. Friends of Hopewell Valley Open Space (FoHVOS), Pennington, NJ. Access 2022.

New York Botanical Garden. Invasive Plants: Emerging Invasive: Corydalis incisa, Early detection, rapid response: applying the resources of the New York Botanical Garden to an emerging invasive species. Mertz Library, New York Botanical Garden, Bronx, NY. Access 2022.

New York Invasive Species Information. Hydrilla. New York Sea Grant Extension Aquatic Invasive Species, Cornell University Cooperative Extension. Access 2022.

North Carolina Extension Gardener Plant Toolbox. *Clematis terniflora*. North Carolina State Extension, NC State University and NC A&T State University. Access 2022.

North Carolina Extension Gardener Plant Toolbox. *Hedera helix*. North Carolina State Extension, NC State University and NC A&T State University. Access 2022.

Okay, J., J. Hough-Goldstein and J. Swearingen. 2010. Least Wanted: Mile-a-Minute, *Persicaria perfoliata*. Plant Conservation Alliance, Alien Plant Working Group, Weeds Gone Wild: Alien Plant Invaders of Natural Areas.

Omernik, J.M. 1987. Ecoregions of the conterminous United States. Map (scale 1:7,500,000). Annals of the Association of American Geographers 77(1):118–125.

Omernik, J.M. 1995. Ecoregions: A spatial framework for environmental management. pp 49–62. In: Davis, W.S. and T.P. Simon (Editors). Biological Assessment and Criteria: Tools for Water Resource Planning and Decision Making. Lewis Publishers, Boca Raton, FL. 415 pp.

Omernik, J.M. 2004. Perspectives on the nature and definition of ecological regions. Environmental Management 34(Supplement 1):S27-S38.

Omernik, J.M. and G.E. Griffith. 2014. Ecoregions of the conterminous United States: evolution of a hierarchical spatial framework. Environmental Management 54(6): 1249–1266.

Ossi, D. 2017. An incisive invader; Invader of the Month: Incised fumewort–*Corydalis incisa*. Maryland Invasive Species Council.

Pannill, P.D., A. Cook, A. Hairston-Strang and J. Swearingen. 2010. Least Wanted: Japanese hop, *Humulus japonicus*. Plant Conservation Alliance, Alien Plant Working Group, Weeds Gone Wild: Alien Plant Invaders of Natural Areas.

Pfingsten, I.A. and N. Rybicki. 2020. *Trapa bispinosa* var. *iinumai* Nakano. U.S. Geological Survey, Nonindigenous Aquatic Species Database (NAS), Gainesville, FL.

Pimentel D., R. Zuniga and D. Morrison. 2005. Update on the environmental and economic costs associated with alien-invasive species in the United States. Ecological Economics 52(3):273–288.

Pimentel, D. 2011. Environmental and economic costs associated with alien invasive species in the United States. pp 411-430. In: Pimentel D. (Editor). Biological invasions: economic and environmental costs of alien plant, animal, and microbe species, 2nd Ed. CRC Press, Taylor & Francis Group, Boca Raton, FL. 449 pp.

Pimentel D., L. Lach, R. Zuniga and D. Morrison. 2000. Environmental and economic costs of nonindigenous species in the United States. BioScience 50(1):53–65.

Port, K. 2014. The Castor Aralia, *Kalopanax semptemlobus*. Arnold Arboretum, Harvard University, Boston, MA. 2 pp.

Randall, J.M. and J. Marinelli (Editors), Brooklyn Botanic Garden (Compiler). 1996. Invasive Plants: Weeds of the Global Garden, Handbook #149. Brooklyn Botanic Garden, Brooklyn, NY. 111 pp.

Rawlings, K.A., R.L. Winston, C.T. Bargeron, D.J. Moorhead and R. Carroll. 2018. New Invaders of the Northeast and Northcentral United States, FHTET-2017-04. U.S. Department of Agriculture, Forest Service, Forest Health Assessment and Applied Sciences Team, Morgantown, WV. 124 pp.

Redman, D. 1995. Distribution and habitat types for Nepal Microstegium [*Microstegium vimineum* (Trin.) Camus] in Maryland and the District of Columbia. Castanea, Southern Appalachian Botanical Society 60(3):270–275.

Regional Invasive Species & Climate Change Management Challenge. Double Trouble: Understanding risks from invasive species + climate change. Northeast RISCC Management, Regional Invasive Species & Climate Change. 2 pp. Access 2022.

Rehder, A. 1940. Manual of Cultivated Trees and Shrubs Hardy in North America, Exclusive of the Subtropical and Warmer Temperate Regions, 2nd Ed. The MacMillan Company, New York, NY. 996 pp.

Reichard, S.H. and P. White. 2001. Horticulture as a pathway of invasive plant introductions in the United States: Most invasive plants have been introduced for horticultural use by nurseries, botanical gardens, and individuals. BioScience 51(2):103-113.

Rhoads, A.F. and T.A. Block. 2007. The Plants of Pennsylvania: An Illustrated Manual, 2nd Ed. Morris Arboretum of the University of Pennsylvania, University of Pennsylvania Press. Philadelphia, PA. 1042 pp.

Rohling, K. 2017. Fact Sheet: Ecology and control of privet species, *Ligustrum spp*. River to River Cooperative Weed Management Area, IL.

Ruhl, H.A. and N.B. Rybicki. 2010. Long-term reductions in anthropogenic nutrients link to improvements in Chesapeake Bay habitat. Proceedings of the National Academy of Sciences 107(38):16566–16570.

Rybicki, N.B. and J.M. Landwehr. 2007. Long-term changes in abundance and diversity of macrophyte and waterfowl populations in an estuary with exotic macrophytes and improving water quality. Limnology and Oceanography 52(3):1195–1207.

Saltonstall, K. 2002. Cryptic invasion by a non-native genotype of Phragmites australis into North America. Proceedings of the National Academy of Sciences, USA 99(4):2445–2449.

Saltonstall, K. 2006. Phragmites: Native or introduced? Integration and Application Network, University of Maryland Center for Environmental Science, Cambridge, MD. 4 pp.

Saltonstall, K. and D. Hauber. 2007. Notes on *Phragmites australis* (Poaceae: Arundinoideae) in North America. Journal of the Botanical Research, Institute of Texas 1(1):385–388.

Saltonstall, K., P.M. Peterson and R.J. Soreng. 2004. Recognition of *Phragmites australis* subsp. *americanus* (Poaceae: Arundinoideae) in North America: Evidence from morphological and genetic analyses. SIDA, Contributions to Botany 21(2):683–692.

Sarver, M., A. Treher, L. Wilson, R. Naczi and F.B. Kuehn. 2008. Mistaken Identity? Invasive Plants and their Native Look-Alikes: an Identification Guide for the Mid-Atlantic. Delaware Department of Agriculture, Dover, DE, and U.S. Department of Agriculture, Natural Resources Conservation Service. 61 pp.

Schmidt, K.A and C.J. Whelan. 1999. Effects of exotic *Lonicera* and *Rhamnus* on songbird nest predation. Conservation Biology 13(6):1502–1506.

Simmons, R.H., W.C. Taylor, M.E. Farrah, J.S. Graham and J.P. Fulton. 2020. Noteworthy Collections: Maryland and Virginia. Castanea, Southern Appalachian Botanical Society 85:277–284.

Simmons, R.H. 2022. Non-native invasive plants of the City of Alexandria, Virginia. City of Alexandria Department of Recreation, Parks and Cultural Activities, Alexandria, Virginia. 9 pp.

Slattery, B.E., K. Reshetiloff and S.M. Zwicker. 2005. Native Plants for Wildlife Habitat and Conservation Landscaping: Chesapeake Bay Watershed. U.S. Fish and Wildlife Service, Chesapeake Bay Field Office, Annapolis, MD. 82 pp.

Smith, S.B., S.A. DeSando and T. Pagano. 2013. The value of native and invasive fruit-bearing shrubs for migrating songbirds. Northeastern Naturalist, Eagle Hill Institute 20(1):171–184.

Stone, K.R. 2009. Morus alba. In: Fire Effects Information System. U.S. Department of Agriculture, Forest Service, Rocky Mountain Research Station, Fire Sciences Laboratory (Producer).

Stone, K.R. 2009. Vinca major, V. minor. In: Fire Effects Information System. U.S. Department of Agriculture, Forest Service, Rocky Mountain Research Station, Fire Sciences Laboratory (Producer).

Stone, K.R. 2009. Wisteria floribunda, W. sinensis. In: Fire Effects Information System. U.S. Department of Agriculture, Forest Service, Rocky Mountain Research Station, Fire Sciences Laboratory (Producer).

Suzuki, D. Top 10 things you can do about climate change. David Suzuki Foundation. Access 2022.

Swearingen, J. and K. Saltonstall. 2010. *Phragmites* Field Guide: Distinguishing Native and Exotic Forms of Common Reed (*Phragmites australis*) in the United States. Plant Conservation Alliance, Weeds Gone Wild. 34 pp.

Swearingen, J. and T. Remaley. 2010. Least Wanted: Chinese Wisteria, *Wisteria sinensis*. Plant Conservation Alliance, Alien Plant Working Group, Weeds Gone Wild: Alien Plant Invaders of Natural Areas.

Swearingen, J. and T. Remaley. 2010. Least Wanted: Japanese Wisteria, *Wisteria floribunda*. Plant Conservation Alliance, Alien Plant Working Group, Weeds Gone Wild: Alien Plant Invaders of Natural Areas.

Tallamy, D. and M. Alfandari. Homegrown National Park: Start a New Habitat. Access 2022.

Tallamy, D.W. 2009. Bringing Nature Home: How You Can Sustain Wildlife with Native Plants, Updated and Expanded. Timber Press, Inc., Portland, OR. 358 pp.

Tallamy, D.W. 2009. Bringing Nature Home: How You Can Sustain Wildlife with Native Plants, Updated and Expanded, 2nd Ed. Timber Press, Inc., Portland, OR. 360 pp.

Tallamy, D.W. 2019. Nature's Best Hope: A New Approach to Conservation that Starts in Your Yard. Timber Press, Inc., Portland, OR. 256 pp.

Tallamy, D.W. 2021. The Nature of Oaks: The Rich Ecology of Our Most Essential Native Trees. Timber Press, Portland OR. 200 pp.

Tewksbury, L., R. Casagrande and A. Gassman. 2002. Swallow-worts. In: Van Driesche, R., B. Blossey, M. Hoddle, S. Lyon and R. Reardon. Biological Control of Invasive Plants in the Eastern United States, FHTET-2002-04. U.S. Department of Agriculture, Forest Service, Forest Health Technology Enterprise Team, Morgantown, WV. 413 pp.

Thompson, L. and M. Imlay. 2011. Control of Invasive Non-native Plants: A Guide for Gardeners and Homeowners in the Mid-Atlantic Region. Maryland Native Plant Society, Silver Spring, MD. 11 pp.

Thompson, J.P. and K. Kyde. 2016. The "nom de plume" of plume grass is: emerging invader; Invader of the Month: *Saccharum ravennae*—Plume grass/Ravennagrass. Maryland Invasive Species Council.

Tiner, R.W. 1987. A Field Guide to Coastal Wetland Plants of the Northeastern United States. University of Massachusetts Press, Amherst, MA. 285 pp.

Tiner, R.W. 1988. Field Guide to Non-tidal Wetland Identification. Maryland Department of Natural Resources, Annapolis, MD, and U.S. Fish and Wildlife Service, Newton Corner, MA. 283 pp.

Tippery, N.P., G.J. Bugbee and S.E. Stebbins. 2020. Evidence for a genetically distinct strain of introduced *Hydrilla verticillata* (Hydrocharitaceae) in North America. Journal of Aquatic Plant Management 58:1–6.

Tu, M. 2002. Element Stewardship Abstract for *Dioscorea oppositifolia* L. syn. *Dioscorea batatas* (Decne) Chinese yam, cinnamon vine. The Nature Conservancy's Wildland Invasive Species Team, University of California, Davis, CA. 10 pp.

U.S. Department of Agriculture, Agricultural Research Service. U.S. National Plant Germplasm System. The GRIN-Global Project (GRIN-Global), Germplasm Resources Information Network (GRIN). Access 2022.

U.S. Department of Agriculture, Animal and Plant Health Inspection Service, Plant Protection and Quarantine (USDA-APHIS-PPQ). 2009. Black Stem Rust/Barberry Program Technical Meeting—Discussion Points, 4700 River Road, Riverdale, MD. 4 pp.

U.S. Environmental Protection Agency. Maps 2013. Level III and IV Ecoregions of the Continental United States. Access 2022.

U.S. Environmental Protection Agency. What you can do about climate change. Access 2022.

U.S. Geological Survey. 2021. Map of Physiographic Provinces of the Mid-Atlantic States. Generated from ArcGIS Online: USGS The National Map: National Boundaries Dataset and US Physiographic Provinces (USGS) by crehak1.

United States, Executive Office of the President [Barack Obama]. Executive order 13751: Safeguarding the Nation from the Impacts of Invasive Species. 5 Dec. 2016. 3 CFR 13751. Revised as of 2017.

University of Delaware Cooperative Extension, Agriculture & Natural Resources, University of Delaware Fact Sheets and Publications: Mulberry weed (Fatoua villosa).

Van Driesche, R., B. Blossey, M. Hoodle, S. Lyon and R. Reardon. 2002. Biological Control of Invasive Plants in the Eastern United States. United States Department of Agriculture Forest Service, FHTET-2002-04. Forest Health Technology Enterprise Team, Morgantown, WV. 413 pp.

Virginia Botanical Associates. Digital Atlas of the Virginia Flora. c/o Virginia Botanical Associates, Blacksburg. Access 2022.

Waggy, M.A. 2010. Hedera helix. In: Fire Effects Information System. U.S. Department of Agriculture, Forest Service, Rocky Mountain Research Station, Fire Sciences Laboratory (Producer).

Wagner, D. 2005. Caterpillars of Eastern North America: A Guide to Identification and Natural History. Princeton Field Guides, Princeton University Press, Princeton, NJ. 512 pp.

Washington State Noxious Weed Control Board. Ravennagrass, *Tripidium ravennae*. Olympia, WA. Access 2022.

Watling J.I., C.R. Hickman, E. Lee, K. Wang and J.L. Orrock. 2011. Extracts of the invasive shrub *Lonicera maackii* increase mortality and alter behavior of amphibian larvae. Oecologia 165(1):153-159.

Weakley, A.S., J.C. Ludwig and J.F. Townsend. 2012. Flora of Virginia. Bland Crowder (Editor). Foundation of the Flora of Virginia Project Inc., Richmond, VA. Botanical Research Institute of Texas Press, Fort Worth, TX. 1572 pp. Also, the Flora App for Android and iOS devices. 2017, updated 2020. Flora of Virginia Project. Richmond, VA.

Weakley, A.S. 2022. Flora of the southeastern United States. University of North Carolina Herbarium, North Carolina Botanical Garden. 2022 pp.

Weaner, L. and T. Christopher. 2016. Garden revolution: how our landscapes can be a source of environmental change. Timber Press, Inc., Portland, OR. 328 pp.

Western New York PRISM: Partnering to Protect Western New York from Invasive Species. Japanese Angelica Tree. Great Lakes Center, Buffalo State, State University of New York, Buffalo, NY. Access 2022.

White, M.R. 2013. Invasive Plants and Weeds of the National Forests and Grasslands in the Southwestern Region, 2nd Ed, MR-R3-16-6. U.S. Department of Agriculture, Forest Service, Southwestern Region, Apache-Sitgreaves National Forests. 245 pp.

Wikipedia: The Free Encyclopedia. 2021. *Pennisetum alopecuroides*.

Williams, S.C., M.A. Linske and J.S. Ward. 2017. Long-term effects of *Berberis thunbergii* (Ranunculales: Berberidaceae) management on *Ixodes scapularis* (Acari: Ixodidae) abundance and *Borrelia burgdorferi* (Spirochaetales: Spirochaetaceae) prevalence in Connecticut, USA. Environmental Entomology 46(6):1329–1338.

Wilson, E.O. 2016. Half-Earth: Our Planet's Fight for Life. Liveright Publishing Corporation, New York, NY. 259 pp.

Winston, R.L., C.B. Randall, B. Blossey, P.W. Tipping, E.C. Lake and J. Hough-Goldstein. 2017. Field Guide for the Biological Control of Weeds in Eastern North America, FHTET-2016-04. US Department of Agriculture, Forest Service, Forest Health Technology Enterprise Team, Morgantown, WV. 331 pp.

Woldemeskel, M. and E.L. Styer. 2010. Feeding behavior-related toxicity due to *Nandina domestica* in cedar waxwings (*Bombycilla cedrorum*). Case Report. SAGE-Hindawi Access to Research, Veterinary Medicine International 2010-818159:1-4.

Zheng, H., Y. Wu, J. Ding, D. Binion, W. Fu and R. Reardon. 2004. Invasive Plants Established in the United States that are Found in Asia and Their Associated Natural Enemies, Vol. 1, FHTET- 2004-05. Chinese Academy of Agricultural Sciences, Institute of Environment and Sustainable Development in Agriculture, Biological Control Laboratory, Beijing, P.R. China; U.S. Department of Agriculture, Forest Service, Forest Health Technology Enterprise Team, Morgantown, WV. 147 pp.

Zheng, H., Y. Wu, J. Ding, D. Binion, W. Fu and R. Reardon. 2005. Invasive Plants Established in the United States that are Found in Asia and Their Associated Natural Enemies, Vol. 2, FHTET-2005-15. Chinese Academy of Agricultural Sciences, Institute of Environment and Sustainable Development in Agriculture, Biological Control Laboratory, Beijing, P.R. China; U.S. Department of Agriculture, Forest Service, Forest Health Technology Enterprise Team, Morgantown, WV. 175 pp.

Ziska, L.H. 2003. Evaluation of the growth response of six invasive species to past, present and future atmospheric carbon dioxide. Journal of Experimental Botany 54(381):395–404.

Ziska, L.H., S. Faulkner and J. Lydon. 2004. Changes in biomass and root:shoot ratio of field-grown Canada thistle (*Cirsium arvense*), a noxious, invasive weed, with elevated CO_2: implications for control with glyphosate. Weed Science 52:584-588.

Zouhar, K. 2009. Euonymus fortunei. In: Fire Effects Information System. U.S. Department of Agriculture, Forest Service, Rocky Mountain Research Station, Fire Sciences Laboratory (Producer).

References and Resources, with links to pdfs and websites, are provided in the digital book at invasive.org/midatlantic/fieldguide.

Index to Invasive Plants

Acer platanoides (Norway maple) 111
Aegopodium podagraria (Goutweed) 151
Ailanthus altissimus (Tree-of-heaven) 112
Akebia quinata (Chocolate-vine, Five-leaf akebia) 125
Albizia julibrissin (Silk tree) 114
Alliaria petiolata (Garlic mustard) 57
Ampelopsis glandulosa var. *brevipedunculata* (Porcelain-berry) 126
Aralia elata (Japanese angelica tree) 88
Arthraxon hispidus (Joint-head grass) 40
Arum italicum (Italian arum) 59
Berberis bealei—see *Mahonia bealei*
Berberis thunbergii (Japanese barberry) 90
Berberis vulgaris (Common barberry) 90
Broussonetia papyrifera (Paper mulberry) 115
Buddleja davidii (Butterflybush) 156
Celastrus orbiculatus (Asian bittersweet) 128
Cenchrus purpurascens (Chinese fountain grass) 41
Centaurea stoebe ssp. *australis* (Spotted knapweed) 61
Cirsium arvense (Canada thistle) 63
Clematis terniflora (Sweet autumn clematis) 130
Corydalis incisa (Incised fumewort) 64
Dioscorea polystachya (Chinese yam) 158
Duchesnea indica—see *Potentilla indica*
Elaeagnus umbellata (Autumn-olive) 92
Epipactis helleborine (Broadleaf helleborine) 152
Erianthus ravennae—see *Tripidium ravennae*
Euonymus alatus (Winged burning bush) 94
Euonymus fortunei (Wintercreeper) 131
Fallopia japonica—see *Reynoutria japonica*
Fatoua villosa (Mulberry-weed) 66
Ficaria verna (Fig buttercup, Lesser celandine) 67
Glechoma hederacea (Ground ivy, Gill-over-the-ground) 69
Hedera helix (English ivy) 133
Hemerocallis fulva (Orange daylily) 70
Heracleum mantegazzianum (Giant hogweed) 153
Hesperis matronalis (Dame's rocket) 71
Humulus japonicus (Japanese hop) 135

Hyacinthoides hispanica (Spanish bluebells) 154
Hydrilla verticillata (Hydrilla) 27
Kalopanax septemlobus (Castor-aralia) 156
Lamiastrum galeobdolon—see *Lamium galeobdolon*
Lamium galeobdolon (Yellow archangel) 154
Lespedeza cuneata (Sericea lespedeza) 73
Leucojum aestivum (Summer-snowflake) 155
Ligustrum obtusifolium (Border privet) 96
Ligustrum ovalifolium (Garden privet) 96
Ligustrum sinense (Chinese privet) 96
Ligustrum vulgare (European privet) 96
Lonicera japonica (Japanese honeysuckle) 137
Lonicera maackii (Amur honeysuckle) 98
Lonicera morrowii (Morrow's honeysuckle) 100
Lythrum salicaria (Purple loosestrife) 74
Mahonia bealei (Leatherleaf mahonia) 102
Microstegium vimineum (Japanese stiltgrass) 43
Miscanthus sinensis (Chinese silver grass) 45
Morus alba (White mulberry) 117
Murdannia keisak (Marsh dewflower) 76
Myriophyllum aquaticum (Parrot-feather) 29
Myriophyllum spicatum (Eurasian water-milfoil) 31
Oplismenus undulatifolius (Wavyleaf basketgrass) 47
Oplismenus hirtellus ssp. *undulatifolius*—see *Oplismenus undulatifolius*
Ornithogalum nutans (Nodding star-of-Bethlehem) 77
Ornithogalum umbellatum (Common star-of-Bethlehem) 77
Paulownia tomentosa (Princess tree) 119
Pennisetum alopecuroides—see *Cenchrus purpurascens*
Perilla frutescens (Beefsteak plant) 79
Persicaria filiformis (Asian jumpseed) 80
Persicaria perfoliata (Mile-a-minute) 138
Phellodendron amurense (Amur corktree) 158
Phragmites australis ssp. *australis* (European common reed) 48
Phyllostachys aurea (Golden bamboo) 50
Phyllostachys aureosulcata (Yellow-groove bamboo) 50
Phyllostachys bissetii (Bisset bamboo) 50
Polygonum filiforme—see *Persicaria filiformis*
Polygonum cuspidatum—see *Reynoutria japonica*
Polygonum perfoliatum—see *Persicaria perfoliata*
Potentilla indica (Mock strawberry, Indian strawberry) 83

Pseudosasa japonica (Arrow bamboo) 50
Pueraria montana var. *lobata* (Kudzu) 140
Pyrus calleryana (Callery pear) 121
Quercus acutissima (Sawtooth oak) 123
Reynoutria japonica (Japanese knotweed) 84
Rhodotypos scandens (Jetbead) 157
Ripidium ravennae–see *Tripidium ravennae*
Rosa multiflora (Multiflora rose) 103
Rubus phoenicolasius (Wineberry) 105
Ranunculus ficaria–see *Ficaria verna*
Saccharum ravennae–see *Tripidium ravennae*
Salvinia molesta (Giant salvinia) 32
Schoenoplectiella mucronata (Bog bulrush) 53
Schoenoplectus mucronatus–see *Schoenoplectiella mucronata*
Scirpus mucronatus–see *Schoenoplectus mucronatus*
Scilla campanulata–see *Hyacinthoides hispanica*
Scilla hispanica–see *Hyacinthoides hispanica*
Spiraea japonica (Japanese meadowsweet) 107
Tovara filiformis–see *Persicaria filiformis*
Trapa bispinosa var. *iinumai* (Two-horned water chestnut) 34
Trapa natans (Eurasian water chestnut) 34
Tripidium ravennae (Ravenna grass) 55
Urtica dioica ssp. *dioica* (European stinging nettle) 86
Viburnum dilatatum (Linden viburnum) 108
Viburnum plicatum (Japanese snowball) 108
Viburnum plicatum var. *tomentosum* (Double-file viburnum) 108
Viburnum setigerum (Tea viburnum) 108
Viburnum sieboldii (Siebold viburnum) 108
Vinca minor (Common periwinkle) 142
Vincetoxicum nigrum (Black swallow-wort) 143
Vincetoxicum rossicum (Pale swallow-wort) 145
Wisteria floribunda (Japanese wisteria) 147
Wisteria x*formosa* (Hybrid wisteria) 147
Wisteria sinensis (Chinese wisteria) 147